PENGUIN
PARADISE IS CL(
and Other

Pieter-Dirk Uys was born in Cape Town in 1945. After graduating from the University of Cape Town in 1968 with a BA in Drama he went to England, where he graduated with Honours from the London Film School in 1972. He returned to South Africa and in 1973 joined the Space Theatre in Cape Town, writing, directing and acting in over fifty productions in two years. Then censorship claimed three plays; he created the Syrkel Theatre Company in order to perform and tour his work throughout the country. His plays include *Faces in the Wall*, *Pity about People*, *Selle Ou Storie* (Same Old Story), *Karnaval*, *The Rise and Fall of the First Empress Bonaparte*, *Die Van Aardes Van Grootoor*, *Hell is for Whites Only*, *Appassionata* and *Panorama*. *Paradise Is Closing Down* was presented at the 1979 Edinburgh Festival and at the Young Vic in London; there were subsequent productions in the United States, and it was filmed for Granada Television in 1980. He has written and performed several revues, including his one-man anti-apartheid revues, *Adapt or Dye*, *Total Onslaught* and *Beyond the Rubicon*, which have been performed many times to people of all colours, cultures and beliefs in non-racial theatres throughout South Africa. Uys has written two books: *No One's Died Laughing* and *P.W. Botha: In His Own Words*. His most recent work includes the revues *Rearranging the Deckchairs on the S.A. Bothatanic* and the controversial *Cry Freemandela*, as well as his new plays *Just Like Home* and *Scorched Earth*.

PIETER-DIRK UYS

Paradise Is Closing Down
and Other Plays

PENGUIN BOOKS

PENGUIN BOOKS

Published by the Penguin Group
27 Wrights Lane, London w8 5TZ, England
Viking Penguin Inc., 40 West 23rd Street, New York, New York 10010, USA
Penguin Books Australia Ltd, Ringwood, Victoria, Australia
Penguin Books Canada Ltd, 2801 John Street, Markham, Ontario, Canada L3R 1B4
Penguin Books (NZ) Ltd, 182–190 Wairau Road, Auckland 10, New Zealand

Penguin Books Ltd, Registered Offices: Harmondsworth, Middlesex, England.

God's Forgotten first published in South Africa by Ad Donker (Pty) Ltd, Johannesburg, in *Theatre One* 1978
Paradise Is Closing Down first published in South Africa by Ad Donker (Pty) Ltd, Johannesburg, in *Theatre Two* 1981
Panorama first published by Penguin Books 1989
This collection first published by Penguin Books 1989

1 3 5 7 9 10 8 6 4 2

Copyright © Pieter-Dirk Uys, 1978, 1981, 1989
All rights reserved

All inquiries regarding performance rights should be addressed to Macnaughton Lowe Representation Ltd of 200 Fulham Road, London, SW10 9PN.

Made and printed in Great Britain by Richard Clay Ltd, Bungay, Suffolk
Filmset in Monophoto Ehrhardt

Except in the United States of America,
this book is sold subject to the condition
that it shall not, by way of trade or otherwise,
be lent, re-sold, hired out, or otherwise circulated
without the publisher's prior consent in any form of
binding or cover other than that in which it is
published and without a similar condition
including this condition being imposed
on the subsequent purchaser

Contents

Foreword vii
God's Forgotten 1
Paradise Is Closing Down 63
Panorama 129
Glossary 187

Foreword

In 1975 I directed a trilogy of my new plays at the Space Theatre in Cape Town, then the only non-racial theatre in South Africa. *Selle Ou Storie* (Same Old Story) had an age restriction that meant it could not be seen by anyone between the ages of two and twenty-one, so the publication of its script was banned by the censors, while *Karnaval* was stopped outright. So I had a play you could see but not read, and a play you could read but not see. *God's Forgotten* survived the onslaught probably because it had an English title and was set in the future ... Today life in South Africa has nearly caught up with the future hinted at in *God's Forgotten*.

Paradise Is Closing Down was written after the first riots of 1976 reached the heart of Cape Town, and was performed at the Grahamstown Festival in July 1977. The play has been revised and is now set in 1988 during the State of Emergency, the daily violence of which, by comparison, makes 1976 look mild.

Official apartheid was baptized in 1948, three years after I was born, and since then the National Party has ruled over me and 30 million other South Africans. I come from Cape Town, and there was always the view and the mountain and the sea – and Robben Island. But one stopped seeing the island because it was political, and wasn't politics a dirty thing and not to be discussed in decent company?

I grew up in Cape Town, and Table Mountain and Robben Island stayed the same; I eventually moved to Johannesburg to take some air and escape that womb with a view. Soon after that, in 1982, they moved Nelson Mandela off the island to Pollsmoor Prison, because he was nearly a superstar in the eyes of the world media, and superstars, suppressed and imprisoned for a quarter of a century he was, had no place on 'supersymbols' like the Alcatraz in Table Bay.

One evening in Johannesburg I saw a short documentary film on SATV that was part of an Afrikaans children's programme.

There was the view and the mountain.

There were the wild flowers and the surf, the wrecks and the lighthouse.

There was no mention of the maximum-security prison, just glowing references to life on the island as a paradise on earth, a gift from God.

A young Afrikaans woman was talking. She was a teacher at the small school of about fifty children belonging to the warders and prison staff.

'I saw this job advertised and I wanted it so much because it's so beautiful here at the Cape. And then when I got the job over forty other applicants . . . I can't now even go over to Cape Town by boat, because I get so seasick and I feel like I'm in a prison . . .'

And behind her was the blue sky and the turquoise sea.

And the panorama.

Pieter-Dirk Uys

God's Forgotten

————————— o —————————

God's Forgotten is a black comedy or a white tragedy
– depending on whose side you're on.

Characters

———————— o ————————

TOSCA BRAND-JANSEN, *the eldest daughter*
SARAH BRAND, *her sister*
ALIZA BRAND, *their younger sister*
IMOGEN, *their father's new wife*
HASTINGS (voice only)

The setting of the play is Excelsior, the home of His Excellency the Hon. J. J. Brand, a South African statesman.

The action takes place in the large living-room in the Cape-Dutch homestead near Cape Town. The furniture is antique Cape-Dutch and includes a large dinner table and chairs. All the furnishings are covered with large white sheets at the start of the play. French windows lead to a patio. A grand piano. Large South African flag. Pierneef paintings. All we see outside the windows is a rough wall, which runs round the house – we cannot see the top of it.

The time is the future in white South Africa.

God's Forgotten was first performed at the Space Theatre, Cape Town, on 22 May 1975, directed by Pieter-Dirk Uys with Esther Van Ryswyk (TOSCA), Christine Basson (SARAH), Lynne Maree (ALIZA), Maralin Vanrenen (GUDRUN, here called IMOGEN) and Blaise Koch (HASTINGS).

Act One

———————— o ————————

Night.
TOSCA: (*Off*) Jackson? Jackson! Mary? (*She enters. Elegantly dressed, carries a bunch of proteas*) Where is everybody? Hastings? I'm at Excelsior. I don't want to be disturbed. The house is in a mess!
(*Slight pause. Then* HASTINGS's *voice fills the room.*)
HASTINGS: The proofs of the SECPOL Review are waiting on your desk. They've just arrived.
TOSCA: Yes, I expected them yesterday.
HASTINGS: The Department says there's been a delay . . .
TOSCA: The proofs can wait. I need time to study them. If I remember correctly, the whole of Chapter Three needed a re-think.
HASTINGS: The Security Blue priority has been extended to embrace all deviations . . .
TOSCA: The whole Maximum-security Clause reads like a KGB handout! You might alert the Bureau that I expect them to submit something a little more original and effective.
HASTINGS: They won't like it.
TOSCA: We'll discuss it all after tomorrow's press conference. I think the Minister should be fully informed, but I want him to have a good rest first.
HASTINGS: Very well.
TOSCA: I heard that, Hastings.
HASTINGS: Heard what?
TOSCA: The little sigh. Don't worry, as from tomorrow we'll be back to normal.
HASTINGS: Hopefully.

TOSCA: We passed some vagrants on the freeway ...
HASTINGS: The corporal has made his report.
TOSCA: No, Hastings, the news of my father's arrival might have been leaked.
HASTINGS: I doubt that ...
TOSCA: There is to be a total security alert. Round up those people and accommodate them.
HASTINGS: Yes, will that be all?
TOSCA: Has Sarah been found?
HASTINGS: No.
TOSCA: Well, find her and tidy her up. I've enough on my hands as it is. Oh, keep your frequency open, I'll discuss the arrangements as they come to mind. But switch off the GM2, I want some privacy.
HASTINGS: I'd rather not do that, Mrs Jansen ...
TOSCA: I am armed, Hastings. (*Pause.*) Oh, Hastings? (*The GM2 has been switched off. She speaks into a walkie-talkie.*) Hastings?
HASTINGS: Yes, Mrs Jansen?
TOSCA: Fax SATV Channel Three. Get that little bald man ... what's his name ... the little one at the head of Current Affairs. Inform him I intend to use my personal hairdresser tomorrow. And suggest that they send the make-up unit on time for a change. I'll be wearing orange and white.
(*During this* SARAH *has entered. Sloppily dressed. Prone to hay fever. Chain-smoker.* TOSCA *becomes aware of her presence. Levels a pistol at her. Pause.*)
TOSCA: I could've shot you ...
SARAH: (*Sniffs*) Flowers?
TOSCA: Sarah?
SARAH: When's he arriving?
TOSCA: I could've shot you!
SARAH: Me too. (*She has a pistol also.*) Stick 'em up, sister. Bang, bang, you're dead.
(*Laughs.* TOSCA *takes the gun from her.*)
TOSCA: What is happening here?
SARAH: You can tell that forever-sighing Hastings I've got my own little gun. Is the thing switched off?

TOSCA: Yes. They've been looking for you all over the place.
SARAH: Yes, I'm sure. Hastings in a panic, my hideous Corporal Vermeulen in a flap. One of his contact lenses is lost again. God, he gets on my damn nerves!
TOSCA: Sarah, where are Jackson and Mary?
SARAH: I was scared. It can become very still here, at Excelsior.
(*Pause. They listen to the silence.*)
TOSCA: This house always gives me the creeps when I'm alone.
SARAH: Don't worry, I'm here with you.
TOSCA: What was that?
(*They listen.*)
SARAH: It creaks a bit. (*Looks at her hands*) Yellow fingers ...
TOSCA: You smoke too much.
SARAH: Yes.
TOSCA: 'One. Two. Three. Four. Five – Father?' I never had the courage to call for him at night. The hours I seemed to spend, staring at the blackness of the open bedroom door, with all the terrorists in Africa waiting for me to take a breath – to call Father. 'One. Two. Three. Four ...' Go on, say it. Father would chase them all away ... And then the old fridge would suddenly give a gurgle in the playroom and my heart would leap into my mouth and smother my breath with its terror!
SARAH: Yes, it always made me feel safe, that funny gurgle ...
TOSCA: I'd pray: 'Dear Jesus meek and mild, have mercy on this little child – and forgive me my sins and keep me safe always.' I so wanted to go to heaven.
SARAH: What for? We are here.
TOSCA: 'Gentle Jesus meek and mild, please forgive this little child ...' and now the old house sighs and groans and I am older and more terrified than ever before.
SARAH: 'One. Two. Three. Four. Five?'
TOSCA: 'Father?' (*Pause.*) He's coming home.
SARAH: I can feel it. Those damn flowers give me hay fever.
TOSCA: He might be in the country already, I don't know.
SARAH: How did he get in?
TOSCA: That's confidential.
SARAH: Submarine!

TOSCA: How do you know?
SARAH: Is there any other way?
TOSCA: (*Calls*) Jackson! (*She starts clearing the sheets off the furniture. This can take some time, as each piece of furniture is uncovered till the rich brown wood dominates.*) I tried to phone you from my car. Hastings has been trying to contact you all day. All we hear on your GM2 is your corporal's radio. Why aren't you at your flat? It's past nine.
SARAH: Already? Another day's gone . . .
TOSCA: The day will come, Sarah, when Father's name won't keep you out of trouble.
SARAH: I want to go out. I like the night air.
TOSCA: It's illegal.
SARAH: Just another one of your 'security measures' . . .
TOSCA: Which protect you, too!
SARAH: I've been here for hours, feels like days. Slept. In your room, then in my room. Hey, the fridge still gurgles. I looked at Aliza's scrapbooks – photos of us posed for history. Father looking so friendly and nice. Who said the camera doesn't lie? Then I went and lay down on Father's bed and dreamt about *braaivleis* in the veld and looking for tortoises under the bushes and singing our South African songs. (*She sings a bit of one.*) And what else did I do? Oh yes, I invaded Father's drinks cabinet. It's really like a who's who in the government: the State President's brandy, SECPOL's gin, the Army's whisky. I gurgled through the whole lot and ended my orgy with a nice glass of sherry – oh yes, our father always has the best taste in the cabinet. And then I very elegantly vomited the whole regime out on to my clothes, and what you see is what I found. One of Ma's things . . .
TOSCA: Sarah. You didn't dare drink out of the State President's bottle, did you?
SARAH: I'm sorry, Tosca, but that's exactly what I did.
TOSCA: But . . .
SARAH: Don't worry, Tosca, we'll top it up with water or pee in the bottle. No one will know the difference. I found my old school uniform. (*Chants*) 'Which is the best school in the land: Berghof, Berghof, Berghof.'

TOSCA: Come here. What on earth is this?
(*She takes something out of* SARAH's *hair.*)
SARAH: It's a hairclip. Leave me alone, Tosca, I was lonely. Forever alone, I had to do something new. Anyway, I wore this that day I won the cup at the Eisteddfod. It's my life, this little relic. No one ever writes about my life; I have to do my own research in the old cupboards!
TOSCA: I don't ask anyone to write all that nonsense about me, Sarah. Please don't attack me about things that I just have to accept as part of the job.
SARAH: But it is nice, isn't it, to 'coo' like a bird of prey in the splintered tops of the trees? The day will come, big sister, when Father's name won't be enough to keep you on the front page of every local newspaper.
TOSCA: Where are the staff! Jackson?
SARAH: I really look a sight in my school uniform.
TOSCA: Don't tell me they saw you like that?
(SARAH *looks to the window quickly. Pause.*)
SARAH: Like what?
TOSCA: Do you hear anything?
(*Pause.*)
SARAH: Er . . . no. What were you saying?
TOSCA: Did any of the black staff see you dressed like that?
SARAH: Unfortunately people don't look any more. How my boys spoilt me; how they always stared. Did I ever tell you about that one history class? I didn't wear a bra to class that day and every boy failed the test on the 1820 British settlers. There's nothing like contours to upstage Sir George Grey. Keeping . . .
TOSCA: Keeping abreast of the times, yes, I know the story.
SARAH: You don't know the story! My little boys knew how to make me feel like a pretty woman. I wonder what happened to all my boys? To me they're all still under sixteen. Good God, some must be married by now, some must have children; some must be bald, some must be dead. I wonder how many of my boys died during the war. You never bothered to find that out for me, you know?

TOSCA: Sarah, Father will be here any minute from now. The house is in chaos. Go and fetch Jackson and Mary. They're probably watching TV in their compound.

SARAH: No.

TOSCA: Sarah, please – I can't get myself to go out to their rooms. You know how I feel about their habits: that stench. It disgusts me. Please?

SARAH: They're on holiday.

TOSCA: Who's on holiday?

SARAH: Jackson, Mary and old Hitler. I signed their papers this morning. They've gone. I told you, I'm alone here, me and my hairclip.

TOSCA: But Father . . .

SARAH: Your security measures were too successful. How was I supposed to know? No one tells me anything. After all, I'm just the weak-minded one, the loony to keep the truth from!

TOSCA: I've never tried to keep things from you . . .

SARAH: Oh, then why can't I drive my own car? That revolting, repulsive Vermeulen gets on my nerves with his constant arse-creeping and those stupid contact lenses that keep falling out. And besides that, Mrs Jansen, he's a rotten driver! I want to drive my own car where and when I like!

TOSCA: Yes, yes . . .

SARAH: Yes, yes. Well, the black slaves have gone home. Shame, it really looks as if we two white princesses will have to play at being handmaids to the big boss!

TOSCA: Will you be quiet! (*Speaks into walkie-talkie*) Hastings? Check in the Excelsior file. Jackson, Mary and . . . (*To* SARAH) what is old Hitler's name?

SARAH: Adolf?

TOSCA: Hastings, there's another old man. We have our own name for him. There's been a misunderstanding here and they've been sent home. I don't know which homeland they belong to. They're probably still on the bus. Get them back. Hastings? Are you there?

HASTINGS: I'm here, Mrs Jansen.

TOSCA: What are you doing?

HASTINGS: Drinking a lukewarm cup of Department coffee, if you really must know.
TOSCA: Poor Hastings. I want those people here immediately.
HASTINGS: Yes; we'll fly them down from wherever they're detained.
SARAH: No! Hastings, don't fly them...
TOSCA: Shhhh. By the way, Hastings, I've found my sister.
HASTINGS: So it seems. Mrs Jansen, her chauffeur...
(TOSCA *breaks the frequency*.)
TOSCA: Don't you ever do that again! Don't interfere when I'm talking to the Department!
SARAH: They mustn't fly them down, please, Tosca! Old Mary'll die. You know how terrified she is of heights.
TOSCA: No one asked you to send them away.
SARAH: They long for their wives, their children, their grandchildren. They're not all as independent as their Miss Tosca; they need to be with their people.
TOSCA: And what do you mean by that?
SARAH: Old Mary cries. She's scared they'll forget her back there in the kraal, in the slum wherever home is. These are people with whom you are playing at being God, Tosca, people who will not forget. Look, if they must be brought back here, OK, but don't let the Department force old Mary to fly. Tosca, old Mary brought us up!
TOSCA: And her son tried to shoot Father.
SARAH: Nonsense, he just wanted to be allowed to see his mother.
TOSCA: With a gun in his hand?
SARAH: You have a gun in your hand!
TOSCA: We took this land with a gun, we will keep it with a gun.
(*Pause.* TOSCA *is busy with her files.* SARAH *looks out of the window.*)
SARAH: How pretty the garden looks in the moonlight. Or is it the searchlight? I walked to the little *braaivleis-laager* in my old school uniform, singing 'Sarie Marais' ever so softly and sweetly, like the old days. But the walls get higher each year. Soon they'll push the sun out forever. The corporal at the West Gate saw me.

TOSCA: Oh lord...
SARAH: Silly little corporal. He's got flat feet, he says, that's why he's here at Excelsior. Poor flat-footed soldier: so young, so pale, so ruthless. Thanks to his flat feet he might live to the ripe old age of thirty. (*Pause.*) Is the thing off?
TOSCA: Yes. Why?
SARAH: No, just asked. (*Takes a letter out of her pocket*) We've got our little flat-footed friend. We're OK.
TOSCA: Sometimes you make me feel very sad.
SARAH: How exhausting for you. Put away your little pistol, Mrs Jansen, we're safe in Excelsior. (*Reads*) 'Cape Town, 14 July 1985...'
TOSCA: What's that?
SARAH: I found it in Aliza's scrapbook. From... Joshua. Who was Joshua?
TOSCA: I don't know. It's none of your business. Put it back where you found it.
SARAH: It was loose at the back. 'Thank you for your lecture notes. I hope I pass.' Joshua? This Joshua died on the island!
TOSCA: I don't know. It really doesn't interest me.
SARAH: (*Reads*) 'I know what you must be up against at home. I understand, but I cannot accept it. We live in a soap-bubble, Aliza. We are friends, we laugh together. I heard about your dinner-party. Everyone enjoyed it. I couldn't have come anyway, but you didn't allow me that excuse. Aliza, you sleep with me and we share the problems your people have created. It means little to me. Offer me your plate, give me your spoon, look me in the face as I eat at your table. Then you are a friend. I'll return the notes soon. We must not see each other. My people regard your visits as white propaganda. Joshua.' How pathetic. It all looked so simple then, 14 July 1985. It was near the end of one life and the beginning of a death. Sometimes I hope it's all going to end in a few minutes. Everything. Then I just say: thank God we'll all be gone and won't have to apologize. No Nuremberg Trials. There'll be no one to see what we left behind.
TOSCA: Go wash your face.

SARAH: Yes. I found some charcoal crayon in the playroom. Gives tired eyes a pretty glow . . .

TOSCA: Sarah, what if Father invites the Cabinet round for a briefing and they see someone's been at their bottles?

SARAH: It's the blacks who steal. Old Mary who brought us up constantly steals from us. We'll say it's the staff. Let me off the hook; and there are many more where they come from.

TOSCA: This room smells funny.

SARAH: Yes, funny, ever since you came in.

TOSCA: Leave me alone, Sarah, you know what I think of you.

SARAH: Nothing?

TOSCA: If only it were that simple.

(*Pause.*)

SARAH: This room is also dead. When Ma died, she took our lives with her.

TOSCA: Rubbish.

SARAH: Remember that time Father nearly remarried and your pathetic howling forced him to cancel everything?

TOSCA: My 'pathetic howling', as you call my concern, had nothing to do with it.

SARAH: I wonder what our lives would've been like with a new ma.

TOSCA: Father doesn't have the time for new 'ma's. Besides, that Scholtz woman was quite wrong for him, and since then I've been proved right – a social climber of the first order and an alcoholic. There'll probably be a reception tomorrow. Depends, of course, on how Father feels . . .

SARAH: That Scholtz woman was here at one of our Sunday *braais*. She looked so damn smart, I thought you'd have a fit or choke on your *boerewors*. She'd have kept him young, Tosca, it's a pity you chased her away, too.

TOSCA: You'll have to ask your Vermeulen to assist with the catering. I'm far too busy. Where will I find the time for that SECPOL Review!

SARAH: You're only his daughter, Tosca, not his wife or his mother. There are things that he may not want from you, no matter how hard you try and force them on to him.

TOSCA: What are you complaining about now?

SARAH: One day something will happen to him or this country and then we'll be on our own. Then there won't be anyone to nervously open doors for you. Then you'll have to spell your name over the GM2, because the world will have forgotten about Tosca Brand-Jansen, Excelsior's pushy guardian angel.

TOSCA: Thank God that losers like you don't run this country. I can just say thank God for small mercies.

SARAH: It's difficult enough not to enjoy my life here. Please don't make me responsible for the reasons for my happiness.

TOSCA: First things first: the catering. All those people. Now, where are the official lists . . .

(*She exits.* SARAH *looks around the room, listening to the silence.*)

SARAH: The wakes, the parties, the burble of elitist conversation. The whitest of lies, morning suits, botanical hats and sport, sport, sport. The great test matches of yesterday: the Bothas play the Smiths, Air Force beats the Navy; white against white. Who needs the outside world if we can do it ourselves. A nation rots while we play sport. *Vrystaat* . . .

(TOSCA *enters with the lists. Uses her walkie-talkie bleeper*)

TOSCA: Hastings, this is Excelsior.

HASTINGS: Yes, Mrs Jansen?

TOSCA: The official guest list for tomorrow, pages eight and nine of the list, will you get it, please? Sarah, wash your face, that stuff ruins your skin . . .

SARAH: Father's little princess. Go wash your little face, Princess, the people are coming . . .

TOSCA: Shhhh.

HASTINGS: I have the pages. There are three Security Blues. They'll need clearance.

TOSCA: Blues? Don't be silly, these aren't Press people, they are the Minister's friends . . . I don't understand, Hastings, who are they?

HASTINGS: Classified information, of course, Mrs Jansen. I'll have to . . . (*Pause.*) Mrs Jansen, I've just been informed of subversion within the safety radius outside Excelsior.

TOSCA: What has that got to do with me?

HASTINGS: SECPOL will be sending reinforcements. The Minister will be brought straight to the Department. He has valuable information.

TOSCA: But he ...

HASTINGS: I just wanted to warn you, Mrs Jansen.

TOSCA: Electrify the main walls.

HASTINGS: That has been done. I'd like to keep your GM2 open, just for safety.

SARAH: No, damn it, is there no privacy left!
(*Pause.*)

TOSCA: Er ... no.

HASTINGS: But Mrs Jansen, open-GM2 procedure is a primary security measure ...

TOSCA: No. If SECPOL does its job properly, there should be no need for the GM2. Thank you, Hastings.
(*Pause.*)

SARAH: Thanks, I hate that thing.

TOSCA: It's for our own safety. I'd better get back to the Department immediately to meet Father ...

SARAH: No, please stay here. Look, Hastings didn't ask you to go, did he? Look, I'll ... I'll find us something nice to eat, put on some music. We have lovely things. What do you fancy? Like at our soirées? You always played your violin.

TOSCA: Why not?

SARAH: Unforgettable, your fiddle.

TOSCA: Our musical evenings were always wonderful ...

SARAH: Good, I'll find us something tuneful but cultured, and then I'll cook you a perfect ... hard-boiled egg!
(*They laugh.* SARAH *sorts the CDs.*)
What is this Security Blue?

TOSCA: Confidential.
(SARAH *sighs, annoyed.*)
Well, Security Blue exists when all forms of Departmental safety measures have been withdrawn. Security Blue suspects are stripped of their GM2 facilities, weapons and guards. 'Unnecessary for the survival of the nation'. I wonder who they are?

SARAH: Don't let's think about them. Hey, I counted fourteen spare bedrooms here today. I thought there were only twelve.

TOSCA: Fourteen.

SARAH: When the communists take over, seven villages can live in our house: the *Laager* Excelsior. Today I seemed to notice the garden for the first time. Father probably bought it as a jigsaw-puzzle, it looks so perfect. The birds must fly over with crossed legs: shame, our perfect piece of paradise.

(*Music:* 'Claire de Lune'. *They listen.*)

What are you thinking?

TOSCA: Nothing.

SARAH: You look lovely when you just sit and think about nothing.

TOSCA: Sarah, find something to do!

SARAH: Last night I actually made a decision. It was so quiet I could hear the beetle eating the stinkwood of Father's big wardrobe. Have you ever lain awake at night and listened to the beetle eat their way through your heritage? It has to be so still that your heartbeats sound like a frantic knocking at the door: and then you hear them – krts, krts, krts . . .

TOSCA: Sarah . . .

SARAH: Sarah Brand made a decision: that should her famous father die, be it only for show, she would lay him out on his big bed, force a few more frowns into his forehead so that he wouldn't look too soft and useless, straighten out his famous wagging finger – maybe even put it on a little wire so that it shakes up and down – and hide a tiny speaker behind his one false tooth: (*In a deep voice*) 'Do not hide away in terror, o my daughters, for your father is home in Excelsior, and all will be well in our land!' We'll ask for a krugerrand or two at the door – a guided tour! Just think, for each excursion you can wear a different colour hat with matching handbag, gloves and smile. View Father in all his splendour, at one with God. United with his Mentor, his Accomplice. Called away to join the Great White God on his segregated cloud to celebrate the triumph of the great South African Dream. Our Father who art then in Heaven, all dead and gone, draped in the flag, our great statesman. Tosca, we could make a fortune! And we'll have

people round us. The empty halls of Excelsior will shimmer in the snot of their sorrow. (*She looks round the room.*) You know, my little flat is so much smaller than this, but just as bare.
(*Breaking glass off.* TOSCA *points her pistol at the window.*)

HASTINGS: Mrs Jansen, your GM2 is operational. Speak from wherever you are.

TOSCA: I'm here.

HASTINGS: There's just been a small incident down at your West Gate. It is now under complete control. A SECPOL squadron has taken over from your military guard. Mrs Jansen, can you hear me?

SARAH: We can all hear you, Hastings! There was a sound of glass breaking outside! Why?

HASTINGS: They threw bottles over the wall. It's all under control.

SARAH: Will you keep GM2 on? For our safety?

HASTINGS: Miss Brand, it's all under control. If you need your privacy, your GM2 can safely be switched off.

SARAH: Sarcastic drip!

TOSCA: Thank you, Hastings. (*To window*) Bottles ... they dare throw their bottles against the walls of Excelsior!

SARAH: Good practice. Bottles tonight, bombs tomorrow.

TOSCA: It's very late. I'd rather you were taken back to your place.

SARAH: I had to escape from there, Tosca.

TOSCA: But Dr Steyn ...

SARAH: To hell with Dr Steyn! Dear God, I'm not an invalid! After all, I was only raped by blacks!

TOSCA: Sarah, don't allow yourself to remember ...

SARAH: How can I forget? Didn't that experience change my life? Look how you treat me, always with a reminder of that moment?

TOSCA: Yes, hate them, but don't destroy yourself!

SARAH: One night, on her way home from Viljoenshof High School, 'Princess Brand', daughter of our great statesman, found herself under a pyramid of Kaffirs and had herself well and truly fucked!

TOSCA: Let's see to the food ...

SARAH: Sarah Brand, defiled by savages. They pushed my face into the dirt of my land and forced their way into me. What a bargain; ten rides on one ticket! How can I forget? The taste of the earth is still fresh on my tongue.

(*Pause.* TOSCA *pretends not to be involved.*)

I was bored, damn it! I did everything and found nothing new in my life. I've seen it all and it stinks. Tosca? I tried to sleep with my Corporal Vermeulen.

TOSCA: Good.

SARAH: You're not listening.

TOSCA: Yes, yes, I'm listening.

SARAH: What did I say?

TOSCA: You tried to sleep with Corporal Vermeulen . . . what?

SARAH: You know, that hideous Vermeulen, sweet seventeen, pimple paradise. Oh, Tosca, please, he was one of the boys from my class at Viljoenshof; still calls me 'miss'.

TOSCA: That I have to waste time like this . . .

SARAH: All he'd do is give his life in defence of my revolting little cage: die for Miss Brand. Come on, where's your sense of humour?

TOSCA: Switch that off, it's getting on my nerves.

SARAH: They're your nerves; switch it off yourself!

(TOSCA *stops the music.*)

Anyway, I made such a fuss, bitching over the GM2, that the Department was forced to give me a permit to come here.

TOSCA: I wonder what Father achieved in Europe. What an incredible breakthrough for us.

SARAH: We had to pass through a raid, sirens shrieking, crawling through the mass, countless fingers clawing at the car windows to escape the horror of being our blacks . . .

TOSCA: We'll probably be televised tomorrow. Father is the first South African to be allowed overseas in over five years.

SARAH: . . . little children, hands outstretched, women wailing, men bleeding next to the road.

TOSCA: Lies!

SARAH: Yes. Lies. No one screamed or clawed at the car or bled. They just stood at the side of the road behind the barbed wire, across from the guns – watching, waiting. Some even smiled. I pressed my face against the tinted glass and cried.

(*Dogs barking and police whistles are heard off.*)
Something's brewing, I can feel it. Another pathetic march with *assegai*, bottle and stick. Our servants stand in protest and we make jokes with the flatfoot soldier while they mow down our masses.

TOSCA: I feel quite ill. I'm not used to sitting still for so long.
(*Pause.*)
SARAH: I can see a grey hair.
TOSCA: Don't worry, I still have enough energy in reserve for a few more years. Let's discuss tomorrow's reception . . .
SARAH: For God's sake . . .
TOSCA: We must do something, Sarah. The silence is driving me mad! We must do something, even if it's only always for tomorrow.
SARAH: I want to watch TV.
(*She switches it on.*)
TOSCA: But Father . . .
SARAH: Shhhh.
(*There follows a scene from a well-known old film. Sentimental. We see them watch, remembering, forgetting. Then suddenly, brutally, the film is interrupted by the United Nations' satellite.*)
TOSCA: Damn!
(*She switches off the TV.*)
HASTINGS: Mrs Jansen?
TOSCA: Yes, Hastings?
HASTINGS: A slight change of plan. Your father has arrived. His motorcade will stop at Excelsior before coming to the Department. The SECPOL Review is being delivered to you by hand. We have a Top Priority rating on it.
TOSCA: Yes, yes.
HASTINGS: By the way, the United Nations' satellite is again jamming SATV with communist propaganda.
TOSCA: Yes, we saw.
HASTINGS: Ruined the best part of the film.
TOSCA: Yes, yes, thank you, Hastings.
HASTINGS: Your GM2 is now operational.
(*Pause.*)

SARAH: I wonder if Father saw Aliza over there. I always think about her, especially here at Excelsior.

TOSCA: She's a traitor.

SARAH: She's our sister!

TOSCA: Traitor! Sold out her country and her people in exchange for her safety.

SARAH: She's free, Tosca.

TOSCA: She's an exile. I don't know her.

SARAH: Then let me remind you: Aliza Brand, Excelsior's little Christian, until one day brotherly love became an illegality and she overnight a traitor. If you may not love your neighbour, Tosca, at least remember your sister.

TOSCA: Don't use the Scriptures to justify her action!

SARAH: We all use the Scriptures to justify our actions!

TOSCA: Be quiet! Go and do something to your appearance. Wasting my time like this. Sometimes you're worse than a snotty-nosed brat!

SARAH: Brat? Mine would've been a black bastard...

(*Sirens and motorcade heard approaching off.*)

TOSCA: He's here!

SARAH: Help me with my hair...

TOSCA: What? We've sat around all night and now you ask?

SARAH: Say I won't be long... For God's sake, he's just my father, what's the matter with me! What must I do? Tell me!

TOSCA: Wash your face, look carefully in the mirror and then you'll know what to do.

(SARAH *exits.* TOSCA *fusses around, prepares to greet her father.* IMOGEN's *voice is heard off.*)

IMOGEN (*Off*): ... of course you know all those stories one hears about lions roaming the streets? With this huge estate outside I can well believe it. Couldn't see much in the dark. I'll drop this in here. (*She enters.*) Oh, hello. What a beautiful old house ... I can't talk, they're waiting for me. Would it be all right if I just left this here? (*A small overnight bag*) I'm Imogen.

TOSCA: Oh?

IMOGEN: Yes.

TOSCA: Good.

IMOGEN: And you're Tosca.
TOSCA: Yes, I know.
IMOGEN: Don't tell me . . . Brand's eldest daughter?
TOSCA: Brand?
IMOGEN: He's waiting in the car. Just stopped by so that this could be delivered to you.
  (*She hands* TOSCA *the SECPOL Review.*)
  Look, I'd better go. He gets so impatient . . .
TOSCA: What?
IMOGEN: We'll be back later and then we can talk. So much to catch up on. But first a meeting with the Cabinet at some Department. It never ends, does it? Politics, politics, right down the line. (*Looks round the room*) Bit musty in here? Anyway, I must run. See you later, Tosca.
TOSCA: I see no need for you to come back.
IMOGEN: Brand will be impossible to live with if I don't . . .
TOSCA: Don't call him that! My father is a great man!
IMOGEN: I know, Tosca. That's why I married him. Bye.
  (*She exits.* TOSCA *stands, stunned.* ALIZA *enters. Pause.*)
ALIZA: Hello, Tosca.
  (*Sirens heard leaving off.*)
  What? You'd better talk louder, my ears still feel blocked . . . maybe I should try and yawn. (*Pause.*) Father told me your husband was killed in the war. Father told me so many things. The last five years sound like a bad TV horror series. (*Pause.*) She might come across as silly, but she's very nervous of all this. She's English, you'll get used to her after a while. He loves her very much. He's getting old, Tosca, he needs youth to help him forget his mistakes.
TOSCA: Don't talk about him in that tone, you little bitch! Old? The day you turned your back on him and ran away, he became old. Because of you – the greatest mistake of his life. Traitor!
ALIZA: That's over now . . .
TOSCA: I remember it so well. Ma was still alive. We didn't know we'd only have her for a few months longer. Imagine what you did to her in her sickly state. You probably killed her!

ALIZA: Cancer killed her.

TOSCA: She was alive. Our windows were full of sun then – no concrete, no soldiers, no tinted glass. We used to walk on the beach at weekends and laugh together. We were complete. And then you crippled us. 'I can't stay with you, my family. It destroys me having to be responsible for so much tragedy around me.' You accused your father of stealing their self-respect, of making them second-class citizens. Little Aliza was not prepared to lose her life for someone else's dream gone wrong!

ALIZA: Yes, I remember – I was young . . .

TOSCA: And so little Aliza sold out her loved ones and killed her mother. She died of a broken heart, Aliza, not cancer!

ALIZA: She was eaten up by cancer. For years! At least she didn't suffer.

TOSCA: Oh yes, you see the suffering of the suppressed so keenly, but the agony in your own family you push aside with ease. After all, family is only just family. So? The publicity helped? Good job in London? Sympathy from the English?

ALIZA: I suppose the publicity helped.

TOSCA: But you see, little sister, you were wrong. We're still here. Excelsior is not a smoking ruin. Nothing has changed, Aliza.

ALIZA: Tinted glass?

TOSCA: For privacy.

ALIZA: Bullet-proof?

TOSCA: We are stronger than ever before. The war, which you no doubt watched on television, just made us stronger.

ALIZA: And so many died.

TOSCA: Yes; we'd just decided to start a family when he was called to duty and I became the most glamorous widow this country has ever seen. Their damn revolution was our own fault. We were always trying to get them to stand on their own feet. It was supposed to make them proud; we hoped it would make them work. Ungrateful fools, they deserved to die! And yet, in spite of their deaths, our deaths, we are stronger than ever before. The fact that you came back proves it.

ALIZA: Proves what?

TOSCA: You had to share in our security. London isn't easy living, is it?

ALIZA: No.

TOSCA: I knew you'd never lose your taste for comfort. You're a true South African, Aliza Brand. And now, if you'll excuse me, I have some work to do. (*Pause.*) Aliza, who *is* this girl?

(SARAH *enters in an uncomfortable dress. Sees* ALIZA.)

SARAH: You've been arrested.

ALIZA: No.

SARAH: You're so thin, you can't be eating properly.

ALIZA: No, I eat.

TOSCA: Aliza?

SARAH: You've been deported.

ALIZA: No.

SARAH: Something's happened to Father! Something we don't know about?

(*Pause.*)

ALIZA: No.

SARAH: Why the pause?

ALIZA: Tosca will tell you.

TOSCA: Tosca's forgotten. Well, we're a bit disorganized this evening. Sarah's given the staff time off.

ALIZA: Old Mary? Is old Mary still here?

TOSCA: I said: nothing has changed. You'll have to help with the catering, Aliza.

(*They giggle.*)

What's so amusing? The place is falling apart and you laugh? What's the matter with you?

SARAH: You and your catering, Tosca. You'll delay the Day of Judgement for the sake of your catering.

TOSCA: He might be hungry! I'll have a quick bath, then we'll all three go to the kitchen. Aliza? You don't look as pretty as I remember. Pity.

(TOSCA *exits with* IMOGEN's *suitcase.* ALIZA *goes towards* SARAH, *happily.*)

ALIZA: Sarah...

SARAH: Shhhh. Hastings?

HASTINGS: Yes, Miss Brand?

SARAH: Would you be so kind as to switch off the GM2? I want to tell someone the story of my life.

HASTINGS: Out of the question, Miss Brand, it's after eleven. You know the law.

SARAH: I watched it being written. Please, Hastings?

HASTINGS: The law...

SARAH: Hastings, the Department would be very intrigued to learn of your after-hours frolics with your young blond lieutenant. (*Pause. Then she laughs.*) Good old blackmail. So much of it around.

ALIZA: What is this?

SARAH: GM2, our guardian angel.

ALIZA: But why at Excelsior? Why here?

SARAH: Don't be shocked, it's a luxury. The Department has a long list of names waiting for their GM2s. The new South African status symbol.

ALIZA: I don't understand...

SARAH: So we can sleep in peace. At least they can hear when someone attacks the house or...

ALIZA: But what about your privacy?

SARAH: Things have changed, Aliza.

ALIZA: What's happened to us, Sarah?

SARAH: We became fat and secure in our comfort. We became dulled through our belief in our survival. We became proud of our self-sufficiency, our arrogance, our power. As Christians we loved them because they had no hope and we hated each other, because we became our own rivals. We encouraged them to dance and rattle their beads hoping it would make enough noise to warn us in time. And after we deprived them of everything that ultimately destroyed us, we bestowed on them the patience to wait for us to frighten ourselves to death. Do you still think of our token black friends?

ALIZA: Mine were never token.

SARAH: Oh? And where are they now? Your eternal Kaffir buddies?
ALIZA: I lost touch.
SARAH: Ah yes. Well, that's what's happened to us, Aliza. We lost touch. (*Loudly*) Hastings? There are six naked men waving things at me! (*Listens: then*) Now, quickly, why are you here? Why did you leave London? What's happening? Are you under Departmental control?
ALIZA: Please, Sarah, you're asking too many questions . . .
SARAH: I don't understand why you're here. You were free.
ALIZA: Yes, quite free.
SARAH: So? Blackmail! How else did the Department get you to leave Britain!
ALIZA: I wanted to come home, that's all.
SARAH: That's all.
ALIZA: Yes, I missed it. You know, the sea, the air, the sun, the karoo, the wine . . . home.
SARAH: Yes.
ALIZA: Yes. That's why I'm here.
SARAH: They didn't force you?
ALIZA: The moment I saw Father, I decided to come home. I couldn't remember why I'd always fought him, even hated him. He's so elegant, so terrifyingly strong. He's the first person I've felt safe with in years. I need that feeling more than freedom.
SARAH: We have wonderful videos of the sea-air-karoo-wine-sun. I'll run some for you tomorrow.
ALIZA: Who wants to see videos! I want to go to the beach tomorrow. it's such perfect weather. You know, I even missed our sea-sand. I used to finger the salt in restaurants and think of the soft warm dust of Sandy Bay. (*Pause*.) Sarah, what've I said?
SARAH: You've made me homesick, too.
ALIZA: Oh for God's sake, don't tell me we still can't go to the beach on Sundays?
SARAH: You still don't seem to realize that things have changed since the war.
ALIZA: The isolation . . .

SARAH: No, before that even...
ALIZA: We heard that after the missile attack on Johannesburg...
SARAH: No, not just commercial air-travel. Beaches, mountains, picnics, drives: we watch them on video. It's safer. Unless you can justify an armoured escort to take you to the seaside and surround you with steel while you paddle. We now have certain hours each day when armed convoys go into the city. No, it's just a precaution, it's quite safe really – but occasionally a stray car is stopped by gangs of young b-b-bl-black men and people are maimed and hurt. (*She tries to control herself*.) Tell me about London.
ALIZA: What? Oh... grey.
SARAH: And Soho?
ALIZA: Soho? Er... also grey...
SARAH: What are the people like? Happy?
ALIZA: Yes. No. I don't know. One has very little contact with strangers nowadays.
SARAH: Paris?
ALIZA: What's happened to all the black staff?
SARAH: Notre-Dame – is it true they blew it up?
ALIZA: Good God, who?
SARAH: The terrorists.
ALIZA: I don't know.
SARAH: But surely the BBC must've been full of it!
ALIZA: No, I don't recall anything about Notre-Dame. Sarah, since I've arrived I've not seen any of our black people. Where are they?
SARAH: That's odd. I distinctly remember an SATV newsflash on my birthday: Notre-Dame gutted by terrorists, then St Peter's, Westminster Abbey...
ALIZA: That's absolute nonsense, Sarah. Father and I went to Westminster Abbey last week. Believe me, the bombings stopped years ago.
SARAH: So, it seems, did our reality. (*Pause*.) Our blacks have a nuclear bomb. Is that absolute nonsense?
ALIZA: How do you mean, a bomb?
SARAH: A bomb! The United Nations' satellite jams our SATV

with this ... Tosca calls it propaganda. The satellite says the blacks have the Bomb. Now, that is absolute propaganda, isn't it? Isn't it?

ALIZA: I don't know, Sarah. I know very little. Please, I'm very confused ...

SARAH: *You're* confused? You've been living in civilization for so many years and you're confused? I'm starving for reality, Aliza. Five years of total isolation somehow drains the imagination and empties the soul of inspiration.

ALIZA: Of course it would.

SARAH: All right then ... what are they saying about us?

ALIZA: You mean, in Europe?

SARAH: Yes, I mean Europe, London, on the BBC, in the Press! What are they saying!

ALIZA: About South Africa?

SARAH: All the bloody left-wing rubbish as always, I suppose: death-camps, riots, chemical warfare ...

ALIZA: Nothing.

SARAH: What do you mean: nothing?

ALIZA: Nothing. Not a word.

SARAH: But we were told ...

ALIZA: That's why I had to come home! Outside in the rest of the world South Africa has ceased to exist. For years I couldn't find a word in the Press, even referring to our white dictatorship, or anything. The official government-in-exile is black and represents that majority. We don't exist any more.

SARAH: Impossible. Our gold and uranium ...

ALIZA: Things have changed. We don't need your gold ...

SARAH: 'We'? *'We'!* For heaven's sake, wake up, wake up! 'We'?

ALIZA: 'They' ... Sarah, for years nothing has come in or gone out of this country!

SARAH: And you're telling me? Don't gloat, little liberal! Ha, you and Father came in!

ALIZA: Yes.

SARAH: So we're not that isolated after all.

ALIZA: I'm not arguing with you, please, Sarah ...

(*Pause.*)

SARAH: Dear God, I'm sorry . . . I didn't touch you, hold you, kiss you . . .
(*They embrace.*)
My darling, why did you come back? At least I kept living through thoughts of you!

ALIZA: At least you took the chance to change things. I ran away, you stayed and fought.

SARAH: Do you really think that?

ALIZA: Of course. You still love your teaching, don't you?

SARAH: Yes, I love it. I still have that, don't I? And my faith in God? I still have that, haven't I? Haven't I! God is still on our side, no matter what happens. Thank you, Hastings, you can make GM2 operational now.

HASTINGS: Yes, Miss Brand.

SARAH: We are white! We are right! We have always been right! Repeat after me, children. The decisions made by our fathers and inspired by God and passed down to us are our true heritage. We will sacrifice all for the truth of our beliefs. We are God's children. We are the only light in a dark world!

ALIZA: Oh my God . . .

SARAH: Behold, they will come with weapons and wealth and enclose you with hatred and darkness, but my love will shine through you. Do not hide away in terror, o daughters of Excelsior, for your father is home, and all will be well with white South Africa!
(*Pause.*)

ALIZA: Sarah, they do have a bomb . . .
(*All the lights go out. Moonlight through the window.*)

ALIZA: What's happened?
(TOSCA *enters.*)

TOSCA: Sarah, where are your matches?

SARAH: Somewhere on the table next to the vase, I think . . .

ALIZA: Is there trouble or something?

SARAH: Got them?

TOSCA: Yes . . . yes . . .

SARAH: Fresh candles in the bottom drawer.

TOSCA: I know . . .

ALIZA: What's going on!
SARAH: Don't mess candlewax on the priceless stinkwood, Mrs Jansen!
TOSCA: Oh, shush...
(*She lights candles.*)
ALIZA: Please don't be so calm. It frightens me even more!
TOSCA: What?
ALIZA: I don't remember this happening before.
SARAH: I told you, Aliza, things aren't what they used to be.
TOSCA: They either dig up cables or blow up pylons and cause temporary disruption.
SARAH: It's an old trick.
TOSCA: It's a damn nuisance.
SARAH: We have our own power supply, but only for emergencies.
ALIZA: Which this isn't?
TOSCA: No. Hastings, can you hear me?
HASTINGS: Yes, Mrs Jansen, your power should be restored in a few minutes.
TOSCA: The pylons are protected by the laser beams. Why did this happen? Who is sleeping on the job?
HASTINGS: It is difficult to keep a check on everyone, Mrs Jansen. After all, there are over 4 million of us.
TOSCA: If it's not restored in five minutes, I'll switch through our own power.
HASTINGS: This is not an emergency...
TOSCA: The Minister will want a meal when he comes home. That's an emergency. Sarah, sit down.
SARAH: I am sitting.
TOSCA: How can an old man... a great man... fall in love with a ... a foreigner overnight? Did you engineer this, Aliza? It smacks of your brand of intrigue.
ALIZA: Oh, stop it.
TOSCA: She will not come into this house as long as I am in charge. 'This room smells musty.' Damn cheek. What's wrong with this room?
SARAH: It smells musty.
TOSCA: Who the hell is this person, Aliza?

ALIZA: Her name is Imogen...
TOSCA: Yes, I know all that. What's she doing here?
ALIZA: Don't tell me you searched her luggage?
TOSCA: Of course I searched her luggage, but it tells me nothing.
SARAH: What are you talking about?
TOSCA: Doesn't she know? Tell her, Aliza!
SARAH: What is it with this Imogen?
ALIZA: Imogen is Father's... er...
SARAH: Mistress!
TOSCA: How dare you say that! Father's a Christian!
SARAH: What has happened without my knowing again? I want to be included in the new decisions!
ALIZA: There are no new decisions, it's just that Father's remarried.
SARAH: Remarried who?
TOSCA: Imogen, for goodness' sake!
SARAH: How can he remarry Imogen? Imogen? Who the hell is Imogen?
TOSCA: She's trying to explain.
ALIZA: Why must I explain? It's got nothing to do with me.
SARAH: A new ma...
TOSCA: She's still a child!
SARAH: ... my God, we've got a new ma!
TOSCA: Explain, Aliza!
ALIZA: All I know is, she met Father ten years ago and suddenly things developed from there.
SARAH: Well I never, there's hope for us yet!
TOSCA: 'Things developed'? Good Lord, Father could be her... father! It's a scandal! And this after all I sacrificed for the family: my husband, my youth, my children...
SARAH: Guess who'll have to play second fiddle now!
TOSCA: You both don't seem to realize what this means!
SARAH: Simple. It means Father will have someone with him.
TOSCA: I'm here.
SARAH: Someone to warm his bed for him when it's cold; you don't qualify. Someone to tell a rude story to; you're too prissy. Someone to help him; you're too keen. And I'll have a new friend. Please God let her be a friend...

TOSCA: I'm sorry but I won't tolerate . . .
ALIZA: Tolerate? You will not 'tolerate' the fact that Father has a life of his own? That he actually enjoys himself when you're not around? No wonder you're all-powerful. I heard odd rumours about your glamorous existence from other South African exiles in London: Tosca Brand-Jansen, our own Evita Peron!
(*She and* SARAH *share the joke.*)
TOSCA: Don't be silly. And where's this girl going to sleep?
ALIZA: They ignore the camps and the homeland fiascos and the anonymous mass of millions waiting above Excelsior's walls like a petrified wave. Who cares about the suffering when you have the glamour of Tosca's latest fashion fad, Tosca's exclusive tea-party . . .
SARAH: *Braaivleis!*
ALIZA: *Braaivleis* . . .
TOSCA: So they talk about me overseas?
SARAH: (*Sarcastic*) They gossip, Sis. Aliza was telling me. You're in every newspaper, like their royalty.
TOSCA: That's going a bit too far. Typical. When will they learn to control their Press?
ALIZA: You're a household name from Brighton to Belfast!
TOSCA: Then the Blockade obviously doesn't work.
ALIZA: It's a failure. The world eats and breathes South Africa.
TOSCA: They need us. They might not understand us, but they cannot ignore us.
ALIZA: You might not understand me, but please don't ignore me . . .
(*The lights snap on.*)
TOSCA: About time.
ALIZA: Tosca?
TOSCA: Yes. (*Snuffs out candles*) So, you're home, Aliza Brand?
ALIZA: Yes.
TOSCA: Father's probably pleased.
ALIZA: Yes.
SARAH: He missed you so.
ALIZA: Did he?
SARAH: Constantly.

TOSCA: Occasionally.
  (*Dogs bark off.*)
ALIZA: Do we still have the dogs?
TOSCA: No, our dogs ran away.
SARAH: I think they were poisoned.
ALIZA: Churchill and Kaiser?
SARAH: Yes, we don't have any animals. I have a kitten at the flat but it always cries. I don't really like it very much.
  (*Pause.*)
ALIZA: What's happened to this room?
TOSCA: Why is everyone suddenly going on about this room? It was painted! Rooms need paint!
ALIZA: No, the feeling in it . . .
TOSCA: All right! It's musty, it's old, it's boring, it's impractical, but it's all we've got! We must make the best of what we have left or else we might as well give up. And I'm sorry, but I don't regard that phrase as part of my vocabulary. Hastings? Have the staff been found?
HASTINGS: Not yet, Mrs Jansen. They'll be transported down. It might take some hours.
TOSCA: Please send me some efficient staff for the night.
HASTINGS: It's very late. I don't know if we can get clearance to enter the townships at this time of night.
SARAH: You're quite right, Hastings. Why lose ten young white lives for the sake of housekeeping?
HASTINGS: That is not what I meant, Miss Brand.
TOSCA: But I must have staff.
ALIZA: Why?
TOSCA: They have to prepare.
ALIZA: What? What do they have to prepare?
TOSCA: The food, the house . . .
ALIZA: We can do that.
SARAH: Yes. Thank you, Hastings, goodbye. We'll cook.
TOSCA: Don't be silly.
ALIZA: What's the problem? There are three of us.
SARAH: And Imogen. Can she cook?
ALIZA: She's English.

SARAH: Oh dear, better leave the cooking to me.
(*She exits.* TOSCA *starts laying the table.*)
ALIZA: I don't know what to talk to you about.
TOSCA: I don't think there's that much to say.
ALIZA: Oh yes, so much ... so much. The last time we were together in this room, there were only two subjects. The Now and the revolution. At varsity we were for the revolution. We entertained blacks; we even slept with them occasionally just to prove to ourselves how liberal we'd become. They hated us for it and we feared them even more. We voted ... Progressive? Was that the name of the party? Yes, we canvassed for that alternative to the bloody revolution. What alternative? A white revolution instead of the black one? Suppress them or love them; live with them? It never occurred to us. And then I left university with its mixed parties and hope and suddenly the liberals became a legend and Excelsior with its power and secrets became the reality. The State President was Uncle Pieter; the Head of the Security Police had a wonderful sense of humour and I really loved him. But I could not separate them and the result of their work. They were all 'good people'. If we'd had Hitlers and Goerings and Stalins amongst us, it would've been easier to hate. But they weren't the great monsters of history. They were warm, loving Christians who believed as implicitly in their god as they did in their great folly. I couldn't hate them and help to destroy them. I had to run away and try to forget them. They poisoned my conscience with their 'goodness'. And yet, in all my years in foreign free lands, I have never met people who in any way compared to the generosity, the warmth, the hospitality of our 'uncles' and 'aunties'. Do you understand what I'm saying?
TOSCA: I wasn't listening.
ALIZA: Tosca, they made a mistake, and you and Sarah and I are stuck with the terrible consequences.
TOSCA: You've been brainwashed by propaganda!
ALIZA: I'm not attacking you.
TOSCA: You are attacking me! You're assaulting me with your 'humanity'! What do you know about this country? You ran

away, years ago. What was wrong then is forgotten now. You have no right to any opinions. We've proved ourselves as a democracy, Aliza. We've been voted back into power, time after time, in spite of puny opposition. Did they ever win an election? A few occasional personality triumphs, but that's not a bad thing. Any good government thrives on a visible opposition. And I'm all for a bit of glamour.

ALIZA: And where's that visible glamorous opposition now?

TOSCA: We whites have no alternative but to stand together.

ALIZA: Forty million of them and 7 million of us?

TOSCA: Yes, if we have to include the coloureds and Indians: 7 million.

ALIZA: Extraordinary how most of the great men who formulated our lifestyle died comfortably in their beds, leaving us holding the chains. Thank God we have no children.

TOSCA: Yes, thank God.

ALIZA: Why didn't you and . . .

TOSCA: We didn't have time.

ALIZA: Yes, the family is a full-time business. Soon we'd all have died out completely: too scared of our world to produce children and too ashamed of our heritage to share it. Maybe that's why they're waiting. They have time and 40 million. They also have a bomb.

TOSCA: Rubbish.

ALIZA: You think rubbish?

TOSCA: Where from?

ALIZA: Open the atlas, put your finger anywhere and from there – the bomb. You play your violin while they set the fuse. Do you still play your violin?

TOSCA: Time permitting. Why?

ALIZA: Forewarned is forearmed.

TOSCA: Jealous. Always making snide remarks about my playing, you and Sarah.

ALIZA: Why should I be snide about your violin? You played very well.

TOSCA: Never mind; I remember one of our soirées. Everyone wanted my encore and just as I prepared to start, you boomed out: 'Oh God, not again!'

ALIZA: I was only a child!
TOSCA: They all laughed at me.
ALIZA: You never forget.
TOSCA: Just remember one thing for the rest of your life, Aliza Brand . . .
ALIZA: All right, I apologize . . .
TOSCA: I stayed and fought while you ran away. I stayed home and prayed when all seemed lost. I cringed at home, hearing shots and screams, and prepared myself to die for what I believe in, while you fled to safety! I also had black friends, but when that day came, I was white and no 'friend' was going to save my life. I defended your home, your childhood, your roots. I lost my youth, my husband, my mother. I stayed; you didn't. So wherever I choose to play my violin in this country, they will listen, because I stayed and fought!

(SARAH *enters with snacks.*)

SARAH: Always politics. Here, eat something, Aliza, you're too thin for a white woman. What've I missed?
ALIZA: Do you ever think about Ma? Sarah? Tosca? We can't forget her. We must talk about her, remember her. It's the only way to keep her from dying.
TOSCA: Leave her in peace. She's dead.
SARAH: I never stop thinking about her.
TOSCA: What for? To feel sorry for yourself?
ALIZA: Tosca, stop being so noble. There's no one here to impress.
TOSCA: Of course I think about her. Not a second passes without the emptiness of her loss hurting me – all day.

(IMOGEN *enters unseen.*)

But that won't help. She won't come back, like you. We must remember, but privately. Father can't hear her name without weeping. Please, for his sake, we mustn't . . .
IMOGEN: I was hoping her memory wouldn't make my life more difficult here. She sounds like quite a person, the first Mrs Brand. You must be Sarah.
SARAH: Yes.
IMOGEN: Your father spoke a great deal of you.
SARAH: We don't get on that well, but he's all right. What did he say?

HASTINGS: Mrs Jansen, I'd like to speak to you in private, please. Mrs Jansen, this is very urgent. I'll clear a frequency to the Minister's study, if you'll take it from there, please!

TOSCA: Later, Hastings, I have a guest.

HASTINGS: Mrs Jansen, I must insist . . .

IMOGEN: Hastings, I thought we'd decided that I should . . .

HASTINGS: Yes, Mrs Brand, but it's really my duty to . . .

IMOGEN: Please!

TOSCA: 'Mrs Brand'? Where is my father?

IMOGEN: I'm afraid your father is dead.

END OF ACT ONE

Act Two

———— o ————

Morning. Bright sunlight. TOSCA *sits in a chair, looking at a box of photos.* IMOGEN *is outside the open doors, against the wall. She has a book in her hand and reads from it. The silence disturbs her.*

IMOGEN: 'It's about a year ago since Father died, isn't it? I remember how cold it was and how it snowed. I thought then that I would never survive his death; and yet now after a year we can talk about it so easily . . .'
(*Dogs bark off. She starts.*)
'I remember Father's funeral, the military band at the graveside and that salute with rifle fire . . .' (*Looks around*) Where the hell is everybody?
(*More barking off.*)
'Oh dear God, when I woke up this morning and saw this flood of sunshine, all this spring sunshine, I really felt so moved and so happy! I felt such a longing to go back home to Moscow . . . I felt such a longing to go back home to Moscow . . . to Moscow . . .'

TOSCA: All that talk of Moscow isn't going to do you much good, you know.

IMOGEN: (*Startled*) Oh, please don't jump out of the darkness at me like that. Moscow?

TOSCA: Yes, going back to Moscow.

IMOGEN: Yes, well, that was Chekhov's idea; nothing to do with me.

TOSCA: Chekhov? At a time like this?

IMOGEN: I was once an actress . . .

TOSCA: I've never heard of you.

IMOGEN: No, why should you. I wasn't very good. I enjoy reading plays more than playing them. I have a photographic memory that stores up the best of other brains. I use their words to prevent myself from going completely mad. You have some lovely books. This can be a very lonely place if you don't know where anyone is. Were you here all the time?

TOSCA: I had work to do.

IMOGEN: All night?

(*The dogs bark again off.*)

I didn't realize you had so many dogs.

TOSCA: No.

IMOGEN: Oh, strays? Can't we feed them?

TOSCA: SECPOL use dogs.

IMOGEN: Oh, yes, the soldiers. I woke up as they left in their trucks. I watched the sun rise over the mountains from my window. Actually, I stood on a chair and could just see over the top of the wall. Do you think your soldiers left their dogs behind?

TOSCA: No. SECPOL treat their dogs well.

IMOGEN: So these must be strays.

TOSCA: Yes, they must be strays. Look, I'm glad we're alone. I think we should talk.

IMOGEN: Not if you're tired.

TOSCA: We don't have much time!

IMOGEN: All right.

TOSCA: My father was under great pressure lately. There were decisions that he had to make, always a choice between two evils. It's obvious that in London . . . the freedom he felt . . .

IMOGEN: We never talked politics. I knew how important it was for him to relax. He loved the theatre . . .

TOSCA: He had no time for the theatre!

IMOGEN: Theatre, opera. We'd always go together, each time he visited London. A friend of mine worked at your embassy before they closed it. We went in a group once to see . . . I think it was a Chekhov. He still said the play should've been in Afrikaans.

TOSCA: My father would never allow us to indulge in trivial things. Besides, life here was different to your theatre and opera and freedom.

IMOGEN: His description of life here was always so vivid and passionate – the colours and the excitement. It always made me want to come and see for myself. So I did . . .

TOSCA: What did he talk to you about? I mean, what could you two have had in common?

IMOGEN: He was honest about his feelings.

TOSCA: My father was a great man . . .

(*A jet flies over the house loudly.* TOSCA *moves away.* SARAH *has entered, carrying a bunch of flowers.* IMOGEN *opens the book and reads.*)

IMOGEN: 'You're so lovely today, you really look most attractive. Masha looks pretty today also, but as for me . . .'

SARAH: 'As for me, I've just got older and a lot thinner . . .'

(*They speak the lines together.*)

SARAH/IMOGEN: 'But today I'm home, I'm free and I feel so much younger than I did yesterday . . .'

SARAH: 'I suppose that whatever God decides must be right and good, but sometimes I really can't help wondering that if I'd married and stayed home, it would have been a much better life for me . . .'

IMOGEN: 'I would've been very fond of my husband!'

SARAH: Incredible! I played Olga at university!

IMOGEN: I played Olga at college!

SARAH: I was far too young.

IMOGEN: So was I. And bad.

SARAH: That's my book . . . I translated it all into Afrikaans as well . . . I've looked for that book everywhere.

IMOGEN: I found it in there.

SARAH: Aren't these beautiful? (*Shows the flowers*) At least they still stay with us.

IMOGEN: I suppose you also found sleep impossible?

SARAH: No, I slept well. I was just scared you'd all be up before me and do things without me.

TOSCA: And what would we do without you?

SARAH: Everything! I also want to take part in all the official weeping and wailing!

(ALIZA *enters wearing her father's dressing-gown. No make-up.*)

SARAH: You know, it's a terrible thing to say, but I often used to pretend he'd died and then plan what I'd do . . . and now suddenly it's all happened and I can't remember what I'd planned . . . come outside, Imogen, it's lovely in the sun. I can't show you a cherry orchard, but we have some very nice things.

TOSCA: Just stay close to the house.

(*Pause*.)

IMOGEN: You translated all this into Afrikaans?

SARAH: Yes. And *The Cherry Orchard* too. Chekhov works beautifully in Afrikaans.

IMOGEN: I suppose he must. There's an amazing similarity between his white Russians and you people . . .

SARAH: Not really. They lost their revolution.

ALIZA: Oh God, I feel so awful. Those pills you gave me were monsters, Sarah.

SARAH: Oh? Well, you slept didn't you?

ALIZA: Where did you get them?

SARAH: Why?

ALIZA: In London people kill each other to get hold of pills like those.

SARAH: Well I never. They just make you sleep. Come for a walk, Aliza?

ALIZA: No.

TOSCA: I couldn't sleep.

IMOGEN: You should've taken one of those pills.

TOSCA: I don't need to take pills!

(*Again a jet screams overhead.* TOSCA *drops some photos.* ALIZA *picks them up slowly.*)

SARAH: Do you remember any more?

IMOGEN: Any more what?

SARAH: The last scene, you know, when the three sisters are left behind all huddled together . . .

(*She leafs through the book.*)

IMOGEN: Er . . . 'How cheerfully and jauntily . . .'

SARAH: 'How cheerfully and jauntily the band is playing. I really feel as if I want to live! (*She puts her arms round* TOSCA *and* ALIZA *as she acts Olga.*) The years will pass and we will all be gone and quite forgotten . . . our faces and voices will be

forgotten and people won't even know that there once were three of us here...
(TOSCA *starts to cry.*)
– but our suffering may bring happiness to those who come after us...'
TOSCA: Father...
ALIZA: Tosca, don't...
SARAH: 'There'll be a time when peace and happiness will reign in this world, and then we will be remembered with kindness and blessed. No, my dear sisters, life is not finished for us yet...' (*Falters*) Tosca, please...
IMOGEN: (*Reads*) 'We're going to live! The band is playing so cheerfully and jauntily – maybe if we wait a little longer, we will find out why we live, and why we suffer ... oh, if only we knew...' (*She is embarrassed by their breakdown. Leafs through the book*) Yes, well, that's the end of it...
SARAH: Cry, Tosca, cry!
TOSCA: Leave me alone!
(*She breaks away from them roughly.*)
SARAH: I just wanted to help.
TOSCA: Well then, get the good cups ready in the kitchen. The people might start arriving at any moment.
SARAH: Oh no, to hell with 'the people'!
TOSCA: Our people always stand together in times of sorrow. They will come now; we must be prepared.
SARAH: And Excelsior will shimmer...
ALIZA: If only we knew.
IMOGEN: But I've told you everything over and over. Your father went into the building and then into the lift...
TOSCA: Mistake! It happened in the street!
SARAH: She was there!
TOSCA: Outside, outside in the street! They can't penetrate into the Department. It happened in the street.
IMOGEN: Brand was inside when it happened.
TOSCA: Are you saying he was assassinated in his office? What do you think this is? The 1960s? The Houses of Parliament? And don't you call him that!

ALIZA: That was his name.
TOSCA: His friends called him J.J.
IMOGEN: I was his wife.
TOSCA: So you call him sir!
SARAH: Please don't fight. Look, I'll make us some tea, anything ... please ...
ALIZA: We'll wait for the television news.
TOSCA: Why should there be news? Father was attacked and murdered by blacks. They will find the assassins, the murderers. No news. He's dead. He died in the service of his country.
IMOGEN: He died in the lift!
TOSCA: Sarah, why don't you take Imogen out of here and show her something nice? After all, she is *your* friend ...
SARAH: Yes, come on, Imogen, I want to show you our famous *braaivleis-laager* ...
(*Behind* TOSCA's *back she indicates drinking and they exit.* TOSCA *paces, preoccupied.*)
TOSCA: Father is dead ... there can be no official lying-in-state. The Department says such a ceremony would be an illegal gathering and constitutes a breach of the Maximum-security Clause. They're right, of course. Let me think ... yes, we must prepare for the funeral. What about our guests? Oh, this terrible thing has happened to me and here I sit without servants. Never mind, I'll worry about that when the time comes ... (*She automatically takes* ALIZA's *cigarette and puffs at it.*) We can all sit outside, it's warm ... What if they want something to eat? No, no, just tea and coffee. How can I get this place in order ... no, mustn't touch anything. Yes, leave everything as he left it. The people will want to come and see it. Everything as it should be. Our lives ... (*Puts out the cigarette*). I'll go and get ready.
(SARAH *and* IMOGEN *enter.*)
SARAH: Why is Father's room locked?
TOSCA: That's none of your business, and anyway, what do you want from there?
SARAH: Something to drink. Give me the key.

IMOGEN: Not if it's too much trouble . . .
SARAH: And whose side are you on? Tosca, give me the key! (*Suspiciously*) What are you two hiding from me? Why is Father's room locked?
TOSCA: Sarah . . .
SARAH: What've you two been talking about?
ALIZA: Nothing, Sarah . . .
SARAH: Well, I'm sorry, but I want to know what's going on!
TOSCA: Go and prepare yourself for the funeral.
SARAH: I'm not going.
TOSCA: The people are on their way . . .
SARAH: I refuse to go. I want a drink first!
IMOGEN: I also could do with a little vodka.
TOSCA: Leave the cabinet alone!
SARAH: A drink, Tosca, not a *coup d'état*!
ALIZA: For God's sake, give me the key . . .
TOSCA: *I'll* get the key . . .
(*She exits. Pause.*)
IMOGEN: It must be the pills. Dry one out. Is there anything I can do? (*Pause.*) Shouldn't we do something to prepare for these people?
ALIZA: Why should there suddenly be people?
IMOGEN: I don't know, I thought Tosca said . . . Maybe we should get a doctor or something?
SARAH: Why? Does someone feel sick?
IMOGEN: I just thought . . . Look, is she all right?
SARAH: No, she's Tosca, the calm, logical one. Tosca won't cry: too strong. Won't allow herself to be merely human. A true Brand. (*Looks around; listens for the GM2*) The thing's probably off. Our little flatfoot corporal is also gone. Everyone suddenly seems to have more important things to do. Strange, I suddenly even miss my hideous Vermeulen . . . but we must all stay calm, mustn't we? After all, it's only a death in the family. We're quite used to that sort of thing . . . (*She smiles at* IMOGEN's *confusion.*) And you just smile and nod or shrug and frown. Don't you understand anything?
IMOGEN: Your father . . .

SARAH: My father died of a heart attack; Tosca's father was assassinated by blacks.

IMOGEN: It was the pressure of the last few weeks. He wasn't young, Sarah . . . there were no blacks.

SARAH: Of course there were blacks! There are always blacks!

IMOGEN: But I was there with him! My God, aren't I ever going to wake up? I just keep telling myself: it's not your fault, Imogen, this is just a bad dream . . .

ALIZA: That's right, the great South African Dream. Hot line to heaven. Our leaders can't afford to slip out and up via mundane heart attacks or other suchlike cop-outs. We have to add others to the Great Leaders' funeral pyre. Throw his bloated corpse from the twentieth floor and then draw the assassins out of the Security Blue file. (*Fingers the flag*) Funny how obsessed we are with colour, hey?

IMOGEN: His heart stopped.

ALIZA: When our mother died, the heart stopped.

(*Pause*.)

SARAH: Did he ever talk about her?

IMOGEN: No.

SARAH: No.

IMOGEN: Aliza made her sound like a very happy person.

ALIZA: That was careless of me.

SARAH: Yes, she forced herself to live the Dream, just for the sake of us children. She played her part very well, like Tosca, always the perfect consort. She died in agony. I'm sure she was glad to go. It really wasn't worth waking up.

IMOGEN: Cancer.

SARAH: Maybe. She was also comfortable with pills; maybe she took too many, I don't care. It's not important. She took a sense of humour with her that left us crippled.

ALIZA: Sarah, enough . . .

SARAH: Yes, enough of Ma. I can't cry about death any more you see, Imogen. The novelty has worn off, and anyway, happy endings don't move me to tears. (*Pause*.) I suppose you've heard about that terrible thing that happened to me? Well, I'm sorry, I can't talk about it; it's too horrible . . . I want to go

home. Hastings? Could you please put me through to my Corporal Vermeulen? Hastings? I know you're there!
ALIZA: Come, Sarah, I'll help you with your hair...
SARAH: What for? I'm not going! Oh, don't look so worried, Imogen, you'll have a wonderful time at the funeral. Tosca will be an example to you all, an opera in herself.
(*She starts off.*)
IMOGEN: Aliza, I'm sure a doctor would...
ALIZA: No!
(*But* SARAH *has heard. She stops and turns.*)
SARAH: We've all got it, like Ma. It's not the *panga* against the head that will end us; it's the cancer inside. Even you have all the symptoms, Aliza Brand: white South African. And now you're in the sanatorium, dying with us, while they wait outside in the perfect sunshine. They won't use their bomb; they won't — but we might. Rather take away what God gave us than share it with the wood-hewers and the water-carriers. I really love my neighbour. Yes, dear our Father, I love my black neighbour in spite of you... it's my white one I loathe!
(*She throws the letter at* ALIZA.) Here. You left it lying around!
(*She exits.* ALIZA *picks up the letter.*)
IMOGEN: How long is this going to last?
ALIZA: Don't you like it?
IMOGEN: Oh, for God's sake.
ALIZA: Till the pills wear off.
IMOGEN: And then?
ALIZA: And then all hell breaks loose in Excelsior. (*Reads*) 'Cape Town, 14 July 1985...' It all looked so simple then. I keep thinking I'm still back in London and that this is just a state of mind — Excelsior. Strange. For all those years there I cared, I planned, I prayed — and now I'm home and all I want to do is sit on the beach and look at the sea. When did the anger end and the sadness begin? Last night? (*Pause.*) My God, he's actually gone and died, the old bastard. What the hell happens now?
(*From off, the strains of* TOSCA *playing her violin:* 'The Last Rose of Summer'. *They listen.*)

ALIZA: Tosca's encore at the end-of-term concert – always 'The Last Rose of Summer'. It's so beautifully warm outside ... (*Shivers*) When I woke up this morning I felt excited and free. At first I couldn't understand what was bothering me, some reason for me not to welcome the sun and smile. Then I remembered what I was, and the sun started to hurt my eyes. We're so complex, aren't we? As complex as the simpleness by which we live: God and Nature. You might not believe this, Imogen, but I'm going to be happy here. I'll find a bubble to float around in and be very happy. Nearly time for the wild flowers. You should see them, Imogen, it's worth organizing an armed escort. Nice change from life; see a bit of nature.

IMOGEN: Wild flowers aren't at the top of my list ...

ALIZA: But nature is on our side, Imogen. God and Nature. The self-sufficient Christian *laager*. Who needs the world? Maybe we are right and they wrong? Well, God and Nature would know.

(TOSCA *starts to play again.*)

IMOGEN: She doesn't seem to have a large repertoire, does she?

ALIZA: No, it's all for show. You don't need more than one of anything for show.

(*She starts to exit.*)

IMOGEN: Please don't leave me! Aliza, please ... tell me about ... er ... this house. About the family. I want to know more.

ALIZA: Are you frightened?

IMOGEN: No, it's just ...

ALIZA: What are you frightened of?

IMOGEN: I don't know, that's the trouble. I don't know. You all make me think I'll be bludgeoned to death behind every bush for a start ...

ALIZA: Possible.

IMOGEN: Please don't ...

ALIZA: Well then, stay away from the bushes.

(IMOGEN *starts to cry.*)

Pull yourself together, Imogen. You're too new around here. You don't yet have the right to cry. You're on your own.

(IMOGEN *controls herself. Pause.*)

GOD'S FORGOTTEN

IMOGEN: Yes. I'm sorry.
  (*Pause.*)
ALIZA: All right. Tell me about your husband.
IMOGEN: Your father?
ALIZA: No, your husband. My father wasn't the sort of man I'd imagine in bed with a young thing like you. Remember, our father was a great man.
IMOGEN: Let me see ... what do you want me to say?
ALIZA: Describe him.
IMOGEN: Good-looking. Very distinguished. Very amusing.
ALIZA: Very amusing?
IMOGEN: Yes.
ALIZA: About what?
IMOGEN: What?
ALIZA: What was he amusing about?
IMOGEN: Oh, his childhood here in South Africa. His parents ... you know ...
ALIZA: No, they died before I was born.
IMOGEN: Oh.
ALIZA: Yes.
IMOGEN: I'm sorry.
ALIZA: Me too.
  (*Pause.*)
IMOGEN: (*Laughs*) Well, last week I made a joke at his expense.
ALIZA: Really?
IMOGEN: Yes.
ALIZA: Tactless.
IMOGEN: No, he loved it.
ALIZA: Did he?
IMOGEN: I think so. He laughed.
ALIZA: Good. What was the joke?
IMOGEN: I said: Yes, I'm marrying you at last, you dirty old bugger.
ALIZA: Damn you.
IMOGEN: He laughed.
ALIZA: Dirty old bugger?
IMOGEN: It was a joke.

ALIZA: If I'd called him that, he would've slapped my face.
IMOGEN: Well, he didn't slap mine.
ALIZA: You weren't his daughter.
IMOGEN: Age didn't matter between us, you know.
ALIZA: I noticed that on the trip out.
IMOGEN: We always had a good laugh.
ALIZA: Good, your husband sounded fun.
IMOGEN: Yes, for that short time he was.
ALIZA: Nice to know.
IMOGEN: Does it matter now?
ALIZA: No. It just makes me sad that he and I never shared a joke. You seem to have had the best of him.
IMOGEN: He seemed to need me. It made me feel . . . important.
ALIZA: Of course.
   (*Pause.*)
IMOGEN: Er . . . I wonder whatever happened to our drinks . . .
ALIZA: She's probably dressing up for the funeral.
IMOGEN: It doesn't really matter. Just something wet. Water?
ALIZA: I'll get you some soda-water. I'm told one shouldn't drink from the taps.
IMOGEN: Don't tell me your aggressive little blacks poison the water supply?
ALIZA: They didn't say that, but one shouldn't take chances. I'm told my fellow South Africans have the habit of committing suicide in the reservoirs and then dissolving into the water supply. It is, to say the least, a bit off-putting?
   (*She exits.* IMOGEN *becomes aware of the silence. Then dogs bark again. She switches on the television. It is an Afrikaans film. We hear the melodramatic soundtrack. She watches for a bit, then switches off. Pause.* SARAH *enters in an ill-fitting black dress.*)
SARAH: You'd better start getting ready.
IMOGEN: What do you . . .
SARAH: Shhhh.
   (*They both listen. Pause. Then* SARAH *shrugs and lights a cigarette.*)
IMOGEN: What should I wear?
SARAH: What do you have that covers true feelings and fears?

IMOGEN: Aliza's getting me some soda-water. My mouth feels so dry.

SARAH: What are you frightened of?

IMOGEN: What's that noise?

SARAH: (*Stiffens*) I don't hear anything.

IMOGEN: No, in here. That scratching sound. There.

SARAH: (*Relieved*) Beetle.

IMOGEN: In the furniture?

SARAH: Maybe that chair, I can't remember.

IMOGEN: Don't they ever stop?

SARAH: Not until the chair's gone, then into the floor. No, I don't suppose they ever stop.

IMOGEN: What will happen to those men they say killed your father?

SARAH: I don't know.

IMOGEN: But surely it will all come out in the trial?

SARAH: If we had trials for every suspect in this country, we'd be like those beetles: we'd never stop. They'll probably disappear and no one will ever know that they even existed. Some other suspects will just take their places.

IMOGEN: Can't they escape?

SARAH: You've been watching too much cable television – where can one escape to? (*Pause.*) Many years ago there was a political prison near here surrounded by water. All references to it have been deleted from the official records, because no one could believe that a political prison would survive for so long in full view of a thriving Christian community. Even then there was no escape, but they were always in the public eye, so to speak. (*Laughs*) I think there is a God, with quite a sense of humour, too.

IMOGEN: I see nothing funny in that story.

SARAH: No, but look at the irony. Here we are, surrounded by walls to keep them out. We're forgotten here in our luxury, trying to escape through culture and fashion and nostalgia. Magnificent white blind horses stampeding into the rusty barbed razor-wire!

(ALIZA *enters and hands* IMOGEN *a glass.*)

IMOGEN: Oh, really Aliza, you shouldn't have bothered . . .
SARAH: But you asked for it.
ALIZA: She's English. They say those things automatically.
  (TOSCA *enters in full imperial mourning attire.*)
TOSCA: Why aren't you dressed?
ALIZA: I'm not going to a fancy-dress ball.
TOSCA: There's been a change of plan. Hastings is sending a convoy of cars. We have fifteen minutes.
SARAH: But what about the people?
TOSCA: Sarah, I've chosen a hat for you to wear.
SARAH: I'm not wearing a hat!
TOSCA: Aliza, go and get ready. And wear comfortable shoes: we'll be walking behind the casket. The plan is as follows: when we come out of the church, we'll follow the gun-carriage down to the heliport. I'll lead the family, accompanied by the State President and Uncle Stefaan . . .
ALIZA: Uncle Stefaan?
SARAH: Head of SECPOL. (*To* IMOGEN) You should hear him tell a van der Merwe joke. Hysterical!
IMOGEN: I don't understand Afrikaans.
ALIZA: What happened to Uncle Koenie?
TOSCA: Uncle Koenie had to retire. Uncle Stefaan is now the Head of Security.
ALIZA: Is Uncle Koenie dead?
SARAH: Oh yes, shame. Living in Switzerland with his numbered bank account and new German wife. He died just in time.
ALIZA: Clever Uncle Koenie.
SARAH: Rich Uncle Koenie.
IMOGEN: Could somebody just tell me what is going on?
ALIZA: We're discussing the funeral . . .
TOSCA: Please stop interrupting! We don't have much time! Sarah and Aliza, stay together. Aliza, few people know of your return — the fewer the better. A helicopter squadron will give us cover in case of any trouble. SECPOL has the entire city under control.
SARAH: But all the 'subversive elements' are bound to have been arrested by now. Aliza, you can be sure Uncle Stefaan never makes a mistake.

TOSCA: They're still looking for the right people.
SARAH: But they must hurry up and find the right people. And quickly too! What's up with our boys? The Minister's murderers must be punished!
IMOGEN: What about me?
SARAH: Goodness, did you kill him?
TOSCA: Yes!
(*Pause.*)
IMOGEN: Where do I fit into this pageant? What about me?
TOSCA: You can go wherever you like. As far as we are concerned, you don't exist.
ALIZA: Tosca ...
IMOGEN: I'm here.
TOSCA: You also killed him. You can go to hell!
SARAH: We're nearly there!
(*Pause.*)
ALIZA: Imogen belongs in the front of the procession with you.
SARAH: It's unimportant who leads, damn it!
TOSCA: I lead!
SARAH: All right, we'll all lead!
IMOGEN: Shut up, you lot. If you really want an analysis of protocol, none of you lead. I lead. I am his widow.
TOSCA: You don't exist.
IMOGEN: I'm his widow. The new Mrs Brand.
TOSCA: You're not even a South African ...
SARAH: Where's my Vermeulen ...
ALIZA: Yes, but Tosca, she does have a point ...
TOSCA: Please! Listen to us, like a bunch of drunk nannies! Please! Yes, I'm sure Imogen has many points in her favour, but we have enough problems and I'm not even prepared to consider any imported ones. Now, if we all listen to me, there'll be no anonymous massacre in the *braaivleis-laager*. We'll get back to the city safely and try and start again from the beginning ...
SARAH: Pills are wearing off ... I need a pill ...
TOSCA: Well, I don't need pills and that's why you need me.
SARAH: I feel so sick ...
TOSCA: Drink.

(*She hands her the glass and some pills.* SARAH *swallows the pills.*)

HASTINGS: Mrs Jansen, your black staff have been intercepted.

SARAH: Old Mary...

HASTINGS: There'll have to be an official inquiry into their papers. They were signed without authority.

SARAH: I signed them! Me!

HASTINGS: Mrs Jansen, could you please control your sister?

SARAH: Tosca, help them...

HASTINGS: They're being taken to Depot ZA556.

TOSCA: Where are our cars?

HASTINGS: Your car is on its way.

SARAH: Where's my hideous Vermeulen?

HASTINGS: Your 'hideous Vermeulen' will be driving you back to the city, Miss Brand.

TOSCA: Hastings, I still haven't had time to study the SECPOL Review, I'm sorry...

HASTINGS: The SECPOL Review has also been shelved.

TOSCA: But...

HASTINGS: Your GM2 frequency is being discontinued. It's a beautiful sunny morning. Enjoy it. The weather report predicts heavy rain on the way.

(*Pause.*)

TOSCA: Hastings?

SARAH: I hate rain...

(*Pause.*)

ALIZA: Do you think our black staff are weeping at the sudden death of their boss?

TOSCA: Of course; they are our friends.

SARAH: Yes, they worship us.

ALIZA: Their families too? Tosca, I believe that you and the late General Jansen didn't spend that much time together, but then no law forced you to live apart.

TOSCA: There are permits for visits.

SARAH: Families are allowed to visit regularly, Aliza. It's not that bad.

IMOGEN: My God, you're fantastic! Even at a time like this you talk about your tiresome politics. You really amaze me.

TOSCA: You'll just have to get used to it, 'Mrs Brand'. It's a way of life.
IMOGEN: Yes, well, I've never been that interested in politics.
ALIZA: Well, Imogen my dear, it's never too late to start.
TOSCA: Here in South Africa we have more than just your congenial British Political Variety Show.
SARAH: Here we have a little problem . . .
ALIZA: . . . it's not going to be the end of the world . . .
SARAH: . . . but at present it tends to rule our every decision.
TOSCA: Life goes on quite happily and no one is starving to death . . .
SARAH: . . . or officially shot on their doorsteps . . .
ALIZA: . . . unless they're tiresome enough to try and find something called self-respect.
TOSCA: And so we talk about it constantly.
ALIZA: And so we don't feel too badly when nothing gets done.
IMOGEN: Thank you very much. I don't want to be involved.
ALIZA: You're completely involved.
SARAH: You're here.
IMOGEN: I came here as his wife.
TOSCA: You have no husband.
IMOGEN: I came here as his wife!
ALIZA: I came here as his daughter.
SARAH: You have no father.
IMOGEN: Look, your ridiculous politics have nothing to do with me.
TOSCA: You're white! You're one of us, whether we like it or not.
IMOGEN: I'm British!
ALIZA: Imogen, there are many who came to this country because the life was easier, the servants cheaper, the sun warmer.
IMOGEN: I came here because of Brand!
ALIZA: And I came because of the sun . . .
IMOGEN: Then what are you talking about!
ALIZA: But don't you see? Those people are also involved. They voted for us against the others. They're also responsible.
IMOGEN: I haven't voted, have I?
TOSCA: You're here, aren't you?

SARAH: Leave her alone. How can we expect her to understand? You're right, Imogen, it's far saner to quote Chekhov. Oh, we know it's fashionable to talk against what we are – that doesn't count. We do it ourselves. But among ourselves. It's not for you to criticize.

IMOGEN: Aliza criticizes!

ALIZA: Of course, I'm home. And in London I defended everything.

TOSCA: Please, we don't have much time.

SARAH: I feel sick...

TOSCA: Don't worry, Sarah. I'll help you look pretty.

(*She starts to go off with* SARAH.)

IMOGEN: Is there anything I should do?

TOSCA: Yes. Dress yourself. The servants are off.

(*She and* SARAH *exit.*)

IMOGEN: Was that meant to be a joke?

ALIZA: Please just do what she says.

IMOGEN: I really didn't come 6,000 miles prepared for a state funeral. What does your church demand of one? Black?

ALIZA: Black?

IMOGEN: You know what I mean.

ALIZA: Our church demands everything of one. Everything! And gets nothing. Shame.

(IMOGEN *exits.* ALIZA *looks at some of the photos.*)

It was once the most important thing in my life: my church. My belief in my god. I actually looked forward to Sundays because I could wear my best and most expensive clothes in which to apologize: sorry that I'm helping to keep Christianity white; sorry that I find the minister's son so pretty that I can't concentrate on what his father is demanding of me. 'Love your neighbour' he said. Well, his pretty son turned out to be gay and the other neighbour black, so where was I after all? Pity you won't understand the service, Imogen. They'll make Father sound like God's gift to mankind – which he was. And we'll all forgive him for what he was and remember him for what he should've been. I might also remember what I was like and forget what I am. 'Dear Jesus meek and mild, please forgive your little child...'

(TOSCA *has entered. Turns on the television. Funeral commentary to muffled drums and marching.*)

ANNOUNCER: And as the casket is solemnly carried out of the church ... there is a hush among the waiting crowds ... a multinational crowd of brotherhood in mourning. The six pallbearers take their places ... the coffin reaches the gun-carriage and is carefully placed on to it. And they've just stepped out of the church into the golden sunshine, a warm, perfect South African day ... the State President and members of his government, accompanied by the daughters of the assassinated statesman. Tosca Brand-Jansen ...

ALIZA: Tosca!

TOSCA: Shhhh ...

ANNOUNCER: ... as usual the symbol of dignity and elegance, followed by her sisters, Sarah and Aliza ... Aliza Brand returned with her father from his historic overseas mission ... they take their places behind the flag-draped casket and slowly start the sad final journey through this beautiful city at the foot of the mountain ...

(TOSCA *switches the television off. Leafs through a* Vogue *magazine.*)

TOSCA: Oh well, it seems we're too late.

ALIZA: I don't believe it ...

TOSCA: Look at this new *Vogue* that Father brought me from London ...

ALIZA: There is no funeral.

TOSCA: No.

ALIZA: You lied!

TOSCA: Yes, I lied. Help me ...

ALIZA: I don't understand. That was me.

TOSCA: No. SATV English Drama Service. The nation must stay calm, that's why a state funeral is necessary. Don't you understand?

ALIZA: Father wasn't assassinated?

TOSCA: No. Heart attack.

ALIZA: Then why is everyone playing this elaborate game?

TOSCA: There's a bit of trouble ...

ALIZA: If there's no funeral, then where are we going?

TOSCA: I know what I'm doing!

ALIZA: Do you get a cheap thrill by dressing up like that?

TOSCA: Don't . . . it helps pass the time. Aliza, we must stay calm.

(*Dogs start to bark. Clouds begin to cover the sun.* TOSCA *leafs through the magazine.*)

These overseas fashions are verging on the pornographic. Thank heavens our people have been spared all this filth . . .

ALIZA: Does Sarah think she's going to a funeral?

TOSCA: Does it matter what she thinks? We must just get her out of here as calmly as possible. This house is her life, our lives . . . if she knew what we know, she'd want to stay and go with it. It's just a matter of time . . . (*Refers to a page*) What on earth is that?

ALIZA: That's a hat.

TOSCA: You're joking.

ALIZA: No, you're joking, Tosca. This has gone far enough!

TOSCA: And please make yourself look respectable. We're not off to a picnic.

ALIZA: My God, I'll do it, even if it kills me . . .

TOSCA: There's trouble . . .

ALIZA: . . . take off my shoes and walk in the sea. Let the icy water caress my knees into numbness. Build a sandcastle. I might even have a picnic: an orange frozen sucker and a packet of chips and I'll watch the lighthouse wink at me from the island. That's what I came home for. I want it!

TOSCA: You'll die out there!

ALIZA: I won't die a liar!

TOSCA: Excelsior has been declared Security Blue.

ALIZA: Excelsior?

TOSCA: We.

ALIZA: But we're Father's family.

TOSCA: Father's dead.

ALIZA: You're one of them. You help make the laws.

TOSCA: Father is dead!

ALIZA: What's that got to do with it? They must protect us.

TOSCA: Why? I helped draft that clause; Security Blue means

switch off and ignore. Security Blue means useless: unnecessary for the survival of the nation.

ALIZA: Survival of the nation? What nation? We are the nation!

TOSCA: Father is dead. Family is just family.

(*The storm approaches. It is murky and dark.*)

It's going to rain. Things always look worse when it rains.

ALIZA: Are you scared?

TOSCA: What for? It's day. 'Five, four, three, two, one – Father?

(*She crumbles.* ALIZA *holds her.*)

Get ready. There's a small service for him in the city. We must go and be seen there and remembered.

ALIZA: Oh God . . .

TOSCA: Don't breathe a word to Sarah. Or whatshername.

ALIZA: Yes, yes . . .

TOSCA: Swear!

ALIZA: I swear . . .

TOSCA: Swear on your mother's soul!

ALIZA: You are scared!

TOSCA: Not a word. Pretend everything's normal . . .

(SARAH's *laughter can be heard off.*)

ALIZA: Normal? And so what's actually become of Father? Dead Father?

TOSCA: Father's up there.

ALIZA: Naturally: halo, wings, the works.

TOSCA: They brought him home early this morning while you were all asleep. He's up there in his room, on his bed. I never realized how small he was. It's better we leave him here in Excelsior. He would've wanted that.

ALIZA: Do not hide away in terror, o daughters of Excelsior, for your father is home and all will be well with white South Africa.

(SARAH *and* IMOGEN *enter in conversation.* IMOGEN *also in black.*)

SARAH: No, actually, I thought it was a plastic bag, or some sort of packet. That's what it looked like in the car's lights, like a plastic bag. I've always enjoyed driving over things like that, plastic bottles and bags, you know – killing them, squashing out their air. There was a concrete rock under it. They must've put it there.

IMOGEN: What for?

SARAH: Old trick, to break the wheel. I could've been killed, you know. There was a terrible spray of sparks as I hit it.

IMOGEN: How fast were you travelling?

SARAH: At first only two of them offered to help. The others were waiting in the dark. They didn't even smile in case the headlamps picked up the white of their teeth.

IMOGEN: I was once driving along the M1 ...

SARAH: I think they were young. Too polite not to be young. Funny, I never thought of them as young till afterwards — their young b-b-bl-black polite bodies. They've also got pink tongues like me ... They didn't hurt me, let me take off my jacket and fold it up. We lay on my beach-towel next to the broken wheel and I even rested my arm against the cool tyre as the hub-cap scratched my shoulder ... scratched my shoulder as they pushed my body up against it with rhythm ... and then the others came ...

TOSCA: Sarah, stop it.

SARAH: And then the others came and it changed and they laughed at me. The nice young ones watched. I suppose that helped. I stared at them, trying to focus on their smiles, while the others did things to me. I forced myself to study their faces so that I wouldn't die and leave you alone with them ...

TOSCA: Take this pill.

ALIZA: What is she saying?

TOSCA: She's drunk. Take this pill, Sarah.

SARAH: They gave me an injection after telling me how dangerous it was to drive alone, but I wasn't alone, was I, Tosca? You see, Imogen, there seemed to be nothing wrong with the car. I must've passed out and then they probably fixed the wheel and even took my beach-towel because it was gone. And my clothes were so beautifully folded that it must've looked funny, I suppose.

IMOGEN: Yes, I suppose so.

ALIZA: And all these years you've forced her to believe she was alone?

TOSCA: It's all wishful thinking . . .

SARAH: And the moral of the story is: always let your cat have a litter before you have her spayed. It gives her fond memories.

(*Pause. A clap of thunder.*)

ALIZA: So you did get at the cabinet after all?

TOSCA: No one is to go into Father's room. Is that understood?

SARAH: No . . . no . . .

ALIZA: How many, Sarah?

IMOGEN: She took some for her headache . . .

ALIZA: How many pills, Sarah!

SARAH: Am I doing it that well?

(*Sound of a siren approaching and a car horn. Thunder.*)

TOSCA: Thank God. Hurry.

SARAH: I've lost my hairclip. It must be somewhere in this room!

TOSCA: Sarah, come on. That's the least of our worries.

SARAH: I want it now! It's mine!

(*She searches.*)

TOSCA: Aliza?

(*But* ALIZA *exits.* TOSCA *sees* IMOGEN *and registers her outfit.*)

What are you wearing?

IMOGEN: A dress . . .

TOSCA: To a funeral?

IMOGEN: I don't really have anything else. *Jammer.*

TOSCA: What?

IMOGEN: *Jammer.* Isn't that Afrikaans for 'sorry'?

TOSCA: Yes. Is that all we've been able to teach you? *Jammer*?

SARAH: (*Searching*) I was here, then I went there . . .

TOSCA: Where did you have that made?

IMOGEN: This? No, I think I bought it in London.

TOSCA: Harrods?

IMOGEN: No, some little shop somewhere. Just off the peg.

TOSCA: Off the peg? I think it's vulgar.

(*She exits.*)

IMOGEN: Yes, maybe you're right . . . (*Finds* SARAH's *clip on the table with the photos*) Is this what you're looking for, Sarah?

SARAH: What?

IMOGEN: This little hairclip?

SARAH: No, I don't even think it's mine. It's silly. (*But she happily puts it into her hair.*) I don't even know your surname.

IMOGEN: It's Brand now.

SARAH: Brand. Morning, Miss Brand. (*Looks at the photos*) Look, I was pretty once, too. You see that small boy? He was so in love with me, can you believe it? Yes, he was in love with *me*! And one morning I found a little note tucked into the class register. 'I love Miss.' A love letter. I still have it at home among my things. I wonder whatever happened to my little secret lover? I can't even remember his name.

IMOGEN: Shouldn't you sit down?

SARAH: Why? Are we staying here now?

(TOSCA *enters*.)

TOSCA: No, we're going back to the city.

SARAH: I don't want to go. The people look at me; they whisper things about me I can't hear. I want to stay in Excelsior!

TOSCA: You'll be safe with me.

SARAH: I don't want to be safe. I want to live!

(ALIZA *enters in casual clothes, carrying* TOSCA's *violin case.*)

ALIZA: Here, your hairclip.

TOSCA: But Aliza . . .

ALIZA: I really don't feel like the Great Drama. I'd rather just go to bed with an Afrikaans book, for old times' sake.

TOSCA: You must come . . . they're everywhere . . .

ALIZA: I'm so tired of running.

(SARAH *is busy with the photos.* TOSCA *talks softly so that she can't hear.*)

SARAH: Aliza, look how terrible you look here. You had jaundice. The picture is all yellow . . . maybe it's old . . .

TOSCA: There'll be no one here.

IMOGEN: I'll be here. She'll be all right.

TOSCA: No, you must come with me.

IMOGEN: You're right about the dress . . .

TOSCA: No, no, the dress is fine . . .

IMOGEN: ... and anyway, I'll feel more at home watching television.

TOSCA: You don't understand Afrikaans.

IMOGEN: I'd like to see what propaganda the United Nations' satellite beams down. Aren't they saying your blacks have a nuclear bomb? Surely that's not true?

TOSCA: No, it's not true. Everything's under control.

ALIZA: Go with her, Imogen.

IMOGEN: I don't think I can face it. Please understand, I don't want to get involved, I don't want to be blamed. Well, maybe I'll join you tomorrow.

SARAH: Tomorrow? 'There won't be a single officer or soldier in the town ... all will just be a memory, and, of course, a new life will begin for us here.' Do you remember the words, Imogen? Olga's words?

IMOGEN: Of course I remember.

SARAH: 'Nothing ever happens as we want it to. I really didn't want to become a headmistress, and yet now I am one. It means we shan't be going to live in Moscow' ... (*She starts whistling 'The Last Rose of Summer.'*) Did you know that there are fourteen spare rooms in this house? The Fortress Excelsior? Three sisters and fourteen spare rooms. And a perfect garden. The sun still makes the grass steam in the early morning. And a *braaivleis-laager*? We really must have a *braaivleis* soon ...

(*She exits to outside.*)

TOSCA: Aliza, please come?

ALIZA: No. We'll stay here. With Father.

(*Pause. Then* TOSCA *speaks with intent.*)

TOSCA: Hastings? Take this urgent memo to SECPOL. Top Security. Chapter Three of the SECPOL Review is totally unacceptable. It's about time you boys did some thinking down there. Initial me for J. J. Brand, Minister of Internal and Foreign Affairs!

(SARAH *appears.*)

SARAH: Come on! Vermeulen's driving us. He's hysterical again, says there's trouble. Hey, he's wearing his spare glasses now, can you believe it? God, he gets so on my nerves, I'd like to smack him one! Come on! (*Looks up*) Oh hell no, here comes the rain!

(*Exits, running.* TOSCA *collects her things, looks at them and exits. Thunder. Rain.*)

IMOGEN: Musty... maybe it's damp...

(*A siren sounds as the car leaves.*)

I suppose if I got the staff to take one room at a time, we might get things moving. And get rid of that beetle. Yes, we'll start with this room.

(*She notices* ALIZA *watching her.*)

It's all so big...

ALIZA: I'm going for a walk.

IMOGEN: A walk? You won't go far, will you?

ALIZA: No, I won't go far.

IMOGEN: But you'll get wet.

ALIZA: I'll be all right.

IMOGEN: Will you?

ALIZA: Oh yes. God is on my side.

(*She starts to go off.*)

IMOGEN: Aliza? Do you think he made me pregnant?

ALIZA: I hope not.

(*She exits into the rain. Pause.* IMOGEN *clears things away. She then turns to the windows with a start.*)

IMOGEN: Aliza?

(*Peers out and closes them. The silence makes her nervous. She switches on the television: a sports programme narrated enthusiastically in Afrikaans. She sits and stares at the television. Then the United Nations' satellite jams the transmission with distortions.*)

THE END

Paradise Is Closing Down

Characters

———————— o ————————

MOLLY
MOUSE
ANNA
WILLIAM

The action takes place in Molly's kitchen in her cottage in Loader Street, Cape Town.

The style is glossy, yuppie-sophistication, with plants and brass and wood. Bright colours. Money.

A sign above the fridge has an arrow pointing to a tin, and the following text:

SWEAR-WORDS R5
BLASPHEMY R10
THE TRUTH R100

A large kitchen table is the centre of the action.

The time is now.

Paradise Is Closing Down was first performed at the Grahamstown Festival on 6 July 1977, directed by Pieter-Dirk Uys with Val de Klerk (MOLLY), Christine Basson (ANNA), Melanie-Ann Sher (MOUSE) and William Meyer (YOUNG MAN): here called (WILLIAM).

The play was rewritten in 1987 with changes.

Act One

———————— o ————————

The kitchen is empty. The radio is on – a news bulletin.

NEWSREADER: And later tonight on our weekly news survey we discuss in depth the current problems in Nicaragua, the Philippines, Northern Ireland and Lebanon, while we also have reports on the plight of the aborigines in Australia and the massacre of the Red Indians in the USA. On the home front we discuss the latest cricket match just ended in Cape Town, as well as the chances that our Miss South Africa has at this year's 'Miss Planet Earth' contest being held in Paraguay.
(MOLLY *enters holding a make-up tray. She sits at the table.*)
This is Radio South Africa, the time is 6.30 . . .
(*She switches the radio off.*)

MOLLY: I'm so sick of politics I could go into lifelong quarantine. Everything about this country is politics, he said. Sex. Homes. Colour. Even death is political, if you can do it in front of a camera in time for the Seven o'Clock News in the US! (*She starts to put on her make-up.*) I don't know why I married him in the first place. I'll never know. I didn't even get used to my new surname before it was all over. 'Politically incompatible: Stephen and Molly'. When in doubt, blame politics: shame, poor little eight-letter scapegoat! Forget that Stephen couldn't get his options up in bed. Oh God, can I forget: 'Hey, Molly, help me, talk dirty . . .' OK, Stephen, poofy-shitty-*poepie-drek* . . . (*Calls*) Mouse? You can imagine what Merle and Graham's decision did for his liberal conscience. He can't believe they're running away. Running away? Rubbish, they made so many nice bucks from the system, now they can move into a mansion in Perth and blame our politics. (*Calls*) Mouse, are you dead?

'The writing's on the wall, Molly,' he said. What wall? He should be so lucky to find something so concrete around here. So OK, the rioting may be on the wall, but who's got the time to read? Give me something real like an earthquake or a tidal wave and I'll also pack the krugerrands and flee, but do I have to write my will every time a stone flies through the air? Do you know he actually had the cheek to *demand* that we put off tonight! What does he want? Us to burn candles for the oppressed and starve? I told him: we're going out and we're going to have a fantastic night and would he please stop wasting my time with his advice and pay my alimony! Bloody cheapskate – 'the end of the world'. He's right, this is Cape Town. So what else is new?

(MOUSE *enters. Her eyes are affected by the tear-gas she encountered earlier in the day. She is exactly as her name suggests: mouse-like.*)

MOUSE: I can't find it.

MOLLY: You didn't look.

MOUSE: I've been looking everywhere. They're so sore, I can scarcely see.

MOLLY: Don't rub your eyes . . .

MOUSE: I used the eyedrops, Molly . . .

MOLLY: Have you looked in all the cupboards?

MOUSE: Yes.

MOLLY: Look in the fridge.

MOUSE: For God's sake . . .

MOLLY: And put that in the tin.

MOUSE: Why?

MOLLY: You said a swear-word. Tin!

MOUSE: Oh for God's sake, Molly!

MOLLY: That's double fine! Pay up – the ex-husband tells me armageddon is just round the corner. Pay up: I want to live!

MOUSE: I don't think that's funny.

MOLLY: Then forgive me for laughing, but, frankly, the thought of plump, middle-aged morning shoppers stampeding down Adderley Street pursued by a bunch of schoolkids with big sticks is rather funny!

MOUSE: How do you know? You were still in bed with those twins.
MOLLY: First taste of tear-gas and they pack their bags and get their visas – shame.
MOUSE: Those twins are too young for you, Molly.
MOLLY: I am not reacting to that personal attack, so you can change the subject, Mouse. Jealousy will get you nowhere.
MOUSE: Well, I was terrified!
MOLLY: If you must stand around a massacre, watching . . .
MOUSE: I was walking to the office. I had to take a tour around the peninsula . . .
MOLLY: Come on, you watched with excitement, just waiting for the blood and guts and dead kids so that you'd have something to tell at the next civil defence tea-party.
MOUSE: There was no massacre . . .
MOLLY: How do you know, if you didn't stand around and watch? Look, take my advice: stay in bed till after the revolution, then you can get a nice job as a char or nanny to ten black brats on the Cape Flats! (*Pause.*) Mousie, come here . . . (*She wipes* MOUSE's *face with a tissue.*) I never thought you could look worse than usual . . .
MOUSE: The girls at the office carry guns now . . .
MOLLY: So who did you take on your tour? I didn't think tourists came here any more.
MOUSE: Six American businessmen. They're here to invest.
MOLLY: Yes, that makes sense. Blow your nose.
(MOUSE *does.*)
You'll live. Now, where is it? I had them on last night. The one was in the bathroom, the other shoe must be somewhere in the house. Look in the bathroom.
MOUSE: I looked there, for God's sake . . .
MOLLY: Since when are you so rich to be so glib? If you go on like this, swearing and cursing like a politician, I'll have to wash your mouth out with washing-up liquid!
MOUSE: You said you wouldn't get involved with those twins, Molly. They're younger than me!
MOLLY: And don't lecture me, Mouse. You're not my mother!
(*She exits.*)

ACT ONE

MOUSE: I can't imagine what you do with them both. Molly? (*Then mutters*) If you had a chandelier, you'd probably swing upside-down with a rose in your bum...
(*She gets the giggles.*)
MOLLY: (*Off*) I heard that, you kinky bitch!
MOUSE: Don't you have other shoes?
MOLLY: (*Off*) Bet your arse!
MOUSE: You said 'arse'!
MOLLY: (*Off*) So did you!
MOUSE: I'll have to owe the tin...
MOLLY: (*Off*) You're a foul-mouthed virgin and I'll write to your poor mother!
MOUSE: My mother's dead...
MOLLY: (*Off*) What?
MOUSE: Was there anything on the news about this morning's riot? Molly?
MOLLY: (*Off*) I'm busy, Mouse; just play with yourself for a bit...
(*Pause.*)
MOUSE: One hears about things like that, but you never expect to see it with your own eyes. They were all so young, the black kids and the white soldiers. All playing cowboys and Indians. They seemed to be enjoying themselves. On a killing spree. I remember things happening in Rhodesia in the old days — my father had a friend who used to keep his money in a purse made of a black man's ball ... er ... you know ... but the children? They were laughing as they were being arrested. Some were bleeding. I really give up.
(MOLLY *enters.*)
MOLLY: Very moving speech, and what do you mean 'give up'? That's just what they want! They want to frighten us to death. Not this old soldier. Do you realize what would've happened to me if I'd ever said 'give up'? After all I've been through before you were even born, and did I ever say 'give up'?
MOUSE: It's not the same...
MOLLY: It wasn't easy. When Stephen left me for that teenage tart with a broken arm...
MOUSE: It was wrong that he beat you up.

MOLLY: Wrong? The teenage tart had the broken arm, because Stephen was the doctor, you twit! Which reminds me: he did hit me once . . .
MOUSE: You told me.
MOLLY: I don't remember telling you.
MOUSE: You did. He hit you here . . .
MOLLY: Anyway, look around you . . . go on, what do you see?
MOUSE: Er . . . your kitchen?
MOLLY: Look further!
MOUSE: I don't understand . . .
MOLLY: Mouse, would I have had all this – a cottage, a sports car, alimony, the twins, a maid, a fashion consultancy, the twins, a home computer . . .
MOUSE: The twins?
MOLLY: . . . would I have had all this if I'd ever allowed myself to say 'give up'?
MOUSE: No, Molly, I don't suppose so.
MOLLY: So there, what have I always told you?
MOUSE: Never give up.
MOLLY: You're not just a pretty face.
(*Pause.*)
MOUSE: Molly, I should go home and change.
MOLLY: Why?
MOUSE: I need a bath and to wash my hair . . .
MOLLY: Nonsense, you look fine.
MOUSE: I can't go out in public with eyes like this!
MOLLY: All right, Mouse, leave me! That's friendship for you!
MOUSE: I want to put on a nice dress.
MOLLY: We won't notice the difference. Don't worry, we'll make you the centre of attraction tonight.
MOUSE: Yes, I'll be the youngest.
MOLLY: Bitch.
MOUSE: The tin, the tin, the tin!
MOLLY: Oh, fuck off!
MOUSE: Washing-up liquid!
MOLLY: You're supposed to help me!
MOUSE: Don't shout at me, Molly . . .

MOLLY: You know what a state I'm in! I always get rattled when I see that fink Stephen!
MOUSE: I thought the twins kept you out of your sleep!
MOLLY: Bloody snotty-nosed bitch! (*She opens the fridge and takes out a cool drink. She sees a shoe in the fridge.*) Come and look here, Mouse...
(MOUSE *looks into the fridge.*)
Look!
MOUSE: What?
(MOLLY *takes out the shoe.*)
MOLLY: If this were a snake, you'd be as dead as democracy!
MOUSE: Your shoe in the fridge?
MOLLY: He was happy to exploit the cheap labour and make a disgusting amount of money not so long ago. Now, just because I want to have a night out with my friends, he suddenly behaves like a guru and says, 'But Molly, this is no time for fun!' Men.
MOUSE: You mean Stephen?
MOLLY: I hate men, especially wholesome, brawny, good-looking bastards like Stephen. Screw, screw, screw, and when you eventually come – they go!
MOUSE: Do you really want me to go like this?
MOLLY: Why is it always fine when you go out with someone? But the moment you're married, the guerrilla war starts.
MOUSE: The crack in the wall's getting bigger.
MOLLY: Freudian little thing. It's those damn neighbours with their priceless objects drilled into *my* wall. I just don't know what this street is coming to.
MOUSE: I see they've now got matching His and Hers Mercedes?
MOLLY: You know, when I moved into this cottage back in the days when cash was a commodity, I still had a coloured family living next door. Forget about 'trendy area'; it was the pits. But Mousie, they were as clean as could be wished for. That's where I met Mrs Peters.
MOUSE: You met Mrs Peters when she was living next door?
MOLLY: No, she was out on the Cape Flats. A relative or something. The best maid I've ever had is Mrs Peters. Or was.

She's starting to get so cheeky nowadays. They're all getting whiter by the day.

MOUSE: What was it like living next to them?

MOLLY: A damn sight more predictable than this *drek* lot – white rubbish. Two Mercedes?

MOUSE: Two convertibles.

MOLLY: It's the only thing you can take out of the country and sell overseas. They're probably also running. (*Yells at wall*) White trash!

MOUSE: The husband is with our travel agency.

MOLLY: God help this country!

MOUSE: Is that a prayer?

MOLLY: You can bet your arse!

MOUSE: And that's a fine!

MOLLY: This area had atmosphere then. All right, they stabbed and raped and brawled but, shit, they had life! My family grew up in the most terrifying chaos – bombs, guns, death. But there was life! Did I tell you about my grandmother?

MOUSE: Yes, Molly. Poland. 1943.

MOLLY: It's like yesterday! The agony, the suffering! You kids just don't know how lucky you are – you with your Rhodesia and Anna with her blacks. We had Hitler!

MOUSE: Molly, I must go; I'll never be able to get ready in five minutes.

MOLLY: Flattery will get you nowhere! Oh, what's the point of all this!

MOUSE: Have you bought a new dress for tonight?

MOLLY: All this ridiculous tarting-up – for why? For what? For who!

MOUSE: It was all your idea!

MOLLY: Thanks, blame me again! Always my fault! Pour me some wine, Mouse. No, not in the fridge, that's the good stuff. Costs a bomb. Give me some Rubbish with a touch of Perrier.
(MOUSE *makes the mixture*.)
So? What are you going to wear?

MOUSE: I don't know . . .

MOLLY: You don't know? We've planned this night for weeks and all we've talked about is how we're going to look and turn every man's head in town and suddenly you don't know what to wear? Don't let me down; the Boer's having a thing specially sent down from Johannesburg.

MOUSE: I must look in my wardrobe.

MOLLY: Welcome back, Laura Ashley. That Anna. All the money that relatives in the government can furnish and what does she do? A dreary radio job reading messages to the boys in the Army. 'And here's a message to Johnny who's just shot his third black child in the township. Your mummy sends love, Johnny, and the cat's had little kittens . . .'

MOUSE: How can you say that . . .

MOLLY: I'm not criticizing her; I mean, she's my best friend. It just all came too easy too soon.

MOUSE: Anna's also been through her bit of hell.

MOLLY: Oh, really! What's that got to do with it? She lost her brother in a landmine explosion, I lost half my family in Poland. We've all suffered, but life must go on.

MOUSE: Maybe that's what the riot was about today . . .

MOLLY: It wasn't a riot, it was just a skirmish among bored brats. God, who needs to be told these things by schoolchildren? Have we all become so impotent that the babies now lead the armies?

MOUSE: What does Mrs Peters say?

MOLLY: I know I've said it for years: what we're fighting here is a losing battle. I said it long before the first stone was cast.

MOUSE: So why haven't you left yet?

MOLLY: Don't you start on me, Mouse! Spare me your sarcasm, please . . .

MOUSE: Sarcasm?

MOLLY: I'm as South African as you and I'm proud of it!

MOUSE: I was Rhodesian, remember.

MOLLY: Then why don't you go home?

MOUSE: Because now home is here.

MOLLY: You're the one who's running away, Mouse.

MOUSE: People don't run away, they run towards.

MOLLY: What?

MOUSE: I don't want to talk about it.
MOLLY: Touchy, touchy, you and the Boer. You both are very quick to point fingers, but when I give you some reality, you both clamp up and make a biceps. I'm also here, and by God and the Boers this is where I intend to stay!
MOUSE: What's happened to Mrs Peters, Molly? Is she OK?
MOLLY: Oh yes, I was telling you about the coloured family. So friendly. Not so quiet, but what the hell, that's one thing they had and that was a lust for life. All night! Noise, shouts, fun. I even went next door one Friday night to threaten them with police action if they didn't shut up, and I ended up in their humble kitchen, drinking wine and telling them the story of my life. So? I didn't have a baby after that drink or come out in a rash!
MOUSE: And where are they now?
MOLLY: Probably somewhere on the Cape Flats, rubbing sand out of their eyes, while we rub tear-gas out of ours, and where's the real life gone to? His and Hers Mercedes!

(*The phone rings.*)

I'm not home.
MOUSE: I don't think they heard you.
MOLLY: (*Bellows*) I'm not home!
MOUSE: Shan't I answer it?
MOLLY: Just because it rings?

(MOUSE *picks up the phone.*)

MOUSE: Hello?
MOLLY: God, when I was the doctor's wife the phone never stopped ringing...
MOUSE: Who?
MOLLY: Stephen always went out on house calls, especially with kids who were sick. He was a good man.
MOUSE: Is she OK?
MOLLY: He was a pain in the arse as a husband and a self-centred bastard.
MOLLY: Don't you want to talk to Molly? Yes, the madam?
MOLLY: The madam? Jesus, you make me sound like old Sarah of the brothel up the road.

MOUSE: OK, I'll tell her.
MOLLY: It's a capitalist society: the people are moved out but the whorehouse stays!
MOUSE: Yes . . . bye.
(*She puts down the phone.*)
MOLLY: What's the time?
MOUSE: Mrs Peters was hurt.
MOLLY: How do you know?
MOUSE: A neighbour just phoned. She was hurt in some unrest in the township . . .
MOLLY: Who's in charge here? Why didn't you let me talk to them?
MOUSE: It was just to say Mrs Peters can't come to work on Monday.
MOLLY: I'm so sick of these excuses. There's always some good reason for staying away. 'My old auntie has lost a leg', or 'There was a fire', or 'Flu'! What do I pay her good money for?
MOUSE: You pay her R200 a month.
MOLLY: For half-days and weekends off, *plus* all the food left over *and* my old clothes! It's a gift!
MOUSE: Yes, Molly. I'd better rush.
MOLLY: So rush! I've booked the table for 8.30. Anyway, if you can't get yourself together in under an hour, you shouldn't be allowed out after six. How do I look?
MOUSE: Fine.
MOLLY: Fine? Thanks for nothing!
MOUSE: No, really, Molly, you look wonderful.
MOLLY: Wonderful?
MOUSE: Outstanding.
MOLLY: Outstanding?
MOUSE: I swear to God!
MOLLY: Ten-rand fine!
(*The phone rings again.*)
MOUSE: Shall I answer it?
MOLLY: Whose phone is it? (*She picks it up.*) Yes? No, I'm busy. Who is it? Oh? Checking if I'm pregnant? Wait, I can't talk here . . . I'll take it in the bedroom. (*She puts down the phone.*

PARADISE IS CLOSING DOWN

Picks up a mirror and looks at her face. As she exits, she shouts up) I hate this face! I want another one! Do you hear? *I want another one!*

(*She exits. We see* MOUSE *is dying to pick up the extension and listen, but she doesn't. She clears up dutifully. She lifts the tin and shakes it – it is empty, bar one coin, which rattles.* MOUSE *laughs. She looks to see if the coast is clear, then softly swears*)

MOUSE: Fart. Piss. Shit!

(*A knock on the kitchen door. She gets a terrible fright and drops the tin.*)

Molly? Molly, I must go!

(*Another knock.*)

Yes? Who is it? Molly, there's someone at the kitchen door. (*She listens at the door.*) Who is it? (*No answer. She carefully puts on the chain and opens the door and peers out.*) Yes? Can I help you? Molly!

(*She undoes the chain and opens the door. We see* WILLIAM *outside.*)

You'd better come in, she won't be long ... (*Then* MOUSE *registers that he is coloured.*) Oh ... just wait, I'd better tie up the dog ...

(*She pushes him out and closes the door.*)

Molly! Vicious Alsatian! Come on ... er ... Rambo, box! Horrible vicious dog! (*Then she hears herself. Mutters*) What am I doing?

(*She opens the door.* WILLIAM *comes in. He carries a plastic carrier-bag full of fruit and vegetables.*)

Sorry ... yes, well ... Molly? Is this for Molly? (*She takes the carrier-bag from him. It is heavy.*) You must be from the corner shop ...

(*Before he can react she takes it across the kitchen and heaves it on to the sideboard.*)

What's in here?

WILLIAM: It's vegetables and fruit ...

MOUSE: I didn't know Molly ate sensibly.

(*She looks into the bag.*)

WILLIAM: You live here?
MOUSE: No, heavens. I live in the boarding-house two blocks down. Number fourteen. Molly lives here. She's on the phone. (*Pause.*) Molly?
MOLLY: (*Off*) Leave me alone, I'm doing a figure transplant in here.
MOUSE: That's Molly. She's off the phone now. Maybe it was one of her boyfriends. She has many boyfriends. (*Pause.*) Look, you are from the Corner shop?
WILLIAM: No.
MOUSE: Oh God, I'm sorry . . . here.
(*She picks up the bag and hands it back to him.*)
I don't know where that other place is, but this is not it.
WILLIAM: You mean old Sarah's place?
MOUSE: I wouldn't know. You've got the wrong address.
WILLIAM: Oh?
(*Pause. Then it dawns on her.*)
MOUSE: Oh hell, are you here to see Molly? (*Calls*) Molly? Quick! Wednesday night's happened on Saturday!
WILLIAM: I used to live in this house.
MOUSE: Really? So you do know Molly? Molly! Surprise!
MOLLY: (*Off*) Bugger off!
WILLIAM: No, I don't know Molly . . .
MOUSE: But you said you lived here.
WILLIAM: When I was a kid.
(*Pause.*)
MOUSE: Oh.
WILLIAM: My family lived in this house since . . . oh, forever. Till Molly and you whites were moved in.
MOUSE: No, I'm just passing through. Really.
WILLIAM: Passing through?
MOUSE: I lived in Salisbury . . . now Harare. I work in a travel agent's. I take people round the peninsula on scenic tours. The views are fantastic.
WILLIAM: Oh.
MOUSE: I'm just saving a bit of money, then I'll move on.
WILLIAM: That's nice.

MOUSE: I have a British passport. (*Pause.*) So, what was this place like when you lived here?

WILLIAM: A little more primitive. I'm joking. Let me see ... I can't really remember. There was an open stove. The place always smelt of burning woodfire.

MOUSE: How romantic.

WILLIAM: Maybe. There was a wall there ...

MOUSE: Molly had the whole place redone. It won a prize in *Style* magazine: the Single Woman's Dreamhouse.

WILLIAM: The backyard looks nice.

MOUSE: Molly's patio. When Table Mountain is lit up for Christmas or some festive occasion you can see it from there.

WILLIAM: When we were here it was full of bits of old cars. My pa used to work on cars.

MOUSE: Amazing.

WILLIAM: I've heard a lot about this place, but never been myself. Mrs Peters works here?

MOUSE: Amazing! You know Mrs Peters?

WILLIAM: I was very small, you know. Me and my little brother. There was another brother, but they say he died of diphtheria.

MOUSE: I'm sorry.

WILLIAM: Is there still a little room next door?

MOUSE: Molly's dressing room. She's had a walk-in cupboard made for all her clothes and shoes and hats and things.

WILLIAM: My granny slept in there with all us kids and Auntie Vera. Granny's also dead.

MOUSE: You all slept in that room?

WILLIAM: Not at the same time. Auntie Vera worked nights at the hospital. Granny never slept. Maybe in the day, I can't remember.

MOUSE: Where do you all live now?

WILLIAM: From here we went to a place in town and then, when that house was also declared part of the white area, we settled out in Manenberg.

MOUSE: Oh, yes.

WILLIAM: Have you been out on the Cape Flats?

MOUSE: Only on the way to the airport, but I've been meaning to.

WILLIAM: You mean the coloured and black townships aren't on your sightseeing tours? People fly all the way to South Africa to have their pictures taken in Soweto.
MOUSE: My job isn't political.
WILLIAM: Just the views.
MOUSE: Yes. (*Pause*.) So why are you here?
WILLIAM: I can't stay anyway. I was looking for Mrs Peters.
MOUSE: She's not here. She only does half-days and she's not stayed late during the riots. Molly says it's typical of them, but maybe she can't manage. She was hurt, they say.
WILLIAM: Who?
MOUSE: Someone phoned and said she was hurt in the township. Nothing serious, though.
WILLIAM: Oh good, so she will be back to do the floors tomorrow.
MOUSE: No, she doesn't come on Sunday.
WILLIAM: Of course. The day of rest. I thought Molly was Jewish?
MOUSE: Yes. She escaped from the Nazis.
WILLIAM: Funny.
MOUSE: Funny?
WILLIAM: The Jews escaped from the Nazis to live happily here under apartheid. Funny.
MOUSE: I don't understand . . .
WILLIAM: There's a crack in the wall.
MOUSE: Listen, Molly is very anti- all that. We all are! It's terrible what you people have had to go through.
WILLIAM: Whoever Molly got in to do her Dreamhouse ripped her off. A bad job.
MOUSE: Maybe you can fix it? I mean, one day.
WILLIAM: *Ja*, before I move back here?
MOUSE: Oh, that's funny.
(*Pause*.)
MOLLY: (*Off*) Mouse! Are you talking to yourself? Is that Boer there? Anna, come and show me what you're wearing! Oh shit, why can't I have normal hair like everyone else!
WILLIAM: Sounds just like my old granny.
MOUSE: I'll tell Molly, she'll be delighted.
WILLIAM: Have you been crying? Your eyes . . .

MOUSE: I was caught this morning in the tear-gas.
WILLIAM: How did it feel?
MOUSE: Terrible.
WILLIAM: You get used to it.
MOUSE: You'd better go.
WILLIAM: You're going out tonight?
MOUSE: Celebrating.
WILLIAM: Birthday?
MOUSE: No. Molly's divorce is final, Anna's lost 4 kilos and I've saved the deposit on my air-ticket to London.
ANNA: (*Off*) Where's everyone?
MOUSE: That's Anna, you'd better go.
WILLIAM: OK, but . . .

(MOUSE *goes to the door to the rest of the house. During this* WILLIAM *manages to get to a drawer in the sideboard and open it.* MOUSE *turns and sees him.*)

MOUSE: What are you doing?
WILLIAM: Er . . . checking the woodwork. Also a rip-off.
ANNA: (*Off*) I'm double-parked, hurry up!
MOUSE: Please go!

(*She pushes him out of the kitchen door. He has left the carrier-bag behind.*)

ANNA: (*Off*) Molly? Where are you? I don't want other Mercs reversing into me, so come on! (ANNA *enters.*) Dear God, Mouse, you look like a refugee!
MOUSE: I must go home and change!
ANNA: What's Molly been saying again?
MOUSE: Eh?
ANNA: You've been crying . . .
MOUSE: I was caught in the tear-gas, Anna, it was terrible. There were these children . . .
ANNA: Like it?

(*She twirls around, showing off her dress.*)

MOUSE: It's lovely.
ANNA: I'm still not sure if it has the right effect.
MOUSE: I look at you and I want to kill myself.
ANNA: Good. It cost a fortune. I didn't feel like basic black with the

working diamonds. Give me a drink. Jesus Christ, my mother gets on my nerves! How much in the tin?

MOUSE: A penny.

ANNA: Put me down on tick for the rest of the night. Molly?

MOUSE: You already owe the tin R220,000 and twenty cents!

ANNA: What cost me twenty cents?

MOUSE: Molly? Anna, I've been trying to get away, it's not been easy.

ANNA: Don't tell me the orgy is off?

MOUSE: Molly's having one of her 'nervous breakdowns'.

ANNA: Always when she washes her hair and it goes down the drain.

MOLLY: (*Off*) Who's there?

ANNA: The Boers are here! Come out with your eyes closed and your pants down!

(MOLLY *shrieks with delight off.*)

Why are we doing this thing tonight?

MOUSE: You've lost so much weight, Anna. It shows!

ANNA: It's the high heels: they help.

MOUSE: How much did you pay for that outfit?

ANNA: Last month's alimony and Wednesday's horses. I feel silly dressed up like this.

MOUSE: You look lovely.

ANNA: I'm not so sure I should be seen in public dressed up like this with you and Molly. We'll look like three lesbians.

MOUSE: We will not look like three lesbians! Stop always saying that! You always try to be funny, even when we went out with those guys.

ANNA: Went out with those guys? Good God, my Neanderthal surfer with his knuckles trailing in the dust, your little travelling salesman who was prettier than you, and Molly forever chewing away at her pink-cheeked soldier-boy – and you don't think we looked like three lesbians? Even the guys looked like three lesbians! I'm not going.

MOUSE: It's been planned, Anna . . .

ANNA: I've got that feeling. Red light flashing! Look, Mouse, I don't need any more reasons to feel grim. Every time someone just looks at me, I . . .

(She starts crying. MOUSE is shocked.)
Pour me some Rubbish . . . thanks.
(She drinks.)

MOUSE: Is it something I said, Anna?

ANNA: Whatever happened to that pink-cheeked soldier-boy of Molly's? Don't tell me she had him for breakfast the next morning? Shame – gone the way of all Molly's flesh. Brian.

MOUSE: Henry. He was killed.
(Pause.)

ANNA: He even looked like my brother. Anna's little pink-cheeked brother, also playing Clint Eastwood with the terrorists!

MOUSE: No, Henry was killed in a car smash. He was on drugs or something. Molly says . . .

ANNA: His things arrived back from Pretoria last week – his leather wallet with those snaps of me and Ma and the spaniel. I hid the stuff from Ma, but she found them. And today being what it is, she laid it all out like on an altar – his portrait from school, the certificate with his medal for bravery, the letter of condolence from the State President. Ma showed everyone with such pride. Some consolation prize.
(She blows her nose. MOUSE stares.)
You never knew my brother, hey?

MOUSE: No. Unfortunately.

ANNA: Why 'unfortunately'? You wouldn't've liked him. He was a rough boy: sports, chicks, drinks with his pals. Quite short. Chunky little chap . . .

MOUSE: Anna, let's go and sit inside . . .

ANNA: And yet he was so gentle with children and animals. Loved kids. Wanted kids one day. That's a joke – he was blown up by a bomb set by kids, while he was hunting down kids. What the hell's happening to us?
(MOLLY enters dressed and ready.)

MOLLY: You bitch! That's not a little number from down the road's boutique, that's an original from Paris! I don't like it! The colour's in agony, the cut's too old-fashioned; you're now too thin where it counts and still too fat where it doesn't; your hair looks terrible and you wear make-up like a man. Otherwise it's a great improvement on last week's leather jodhpurs. Right, start with the floors and work your way up! Oh, by the way, one of the twins told me this joke. 'How many white women does it take to change a light bulb?'

ANNA: Two. One to hold the diet Coke and the other to call the maid.
MOLLY: How do you know?
ANNA: You're not still seeing those twins?
MOUSE: They do *everything* together!
MOLLY: Mouse, are you still here?
MOUSE: I've been so busy! There was a guy here . . .
MOLLY: I will not have my private life broadcast to the world! The table's booked for 8.30. Move your arse, Mouse!
MOUSE: OK, OK . . . That's a fine!
ANNA: Let her wear something of yours, we don't have time . . .
MOLLY: I don't lend out my clothes!
MOUSE: I'll be quick!
   (*She exits.*)
MOLLY: And take your carrots or whatever . . . what is all this shit?
ANNA: Don't tell me she's on her vegetarian crusade again. Well then, that does it! I will not go to an expensive steakhouse with a vegetarian and a Jew!
MOLLY: It's just pork, Anna, not meat!
ANNA: But you eat bacon.
MOLLY: That's different!
ANNA: How come?
MOLLY: And Mouse, bring your own hairbrush! She always uses my things. Mouse?
ANNA: I'm parked in their driveway next door.
MOLLY: Fuck them. They've got a Mercedes sports car *each*.
ANNA: Yes, he told me. Mine's the very latest model.
MOLLY: What a pity you can't take it with you.
ANNA: You can.
MOLLY: Yes, to Australia or the USA. I meant to heaven.
ANNA: It's all becoming the same thing.
MOLLY: Anna, you won't believe what Stephen said to me on the phone this afternoon, just after I spoke to you.

ANNA: I've never had the urge to even want to go and live somewhere else.

MOLLY: He phones up and, sweet as a choirboy, asks if he can come over and have a bath!

ANNA: Maybe if I had kids, one would plan with them in mind...

MOLLY: A bath? I said, 'Listen, you unmentionable bastard, we are now divorced! It is over! Go piss in someone else's bathwater!'

ANNA: ... maybe, but I'm not prepared to start all over again somewhere else. And for what?

MOLLY: What?

ANNA: For what?

MOLLY: A bath!

ANNA: Hey?

MOLLY: I mean, who the hell do they think I am? Some teenage divorcee panting for a reconciliation? Like hell: I've lived! I've been through the armpit of life ten times over and I've learnt the hard way, my dear, and I don't need you or men or anyone!

ANNA: Bye.

(*She makes for the door.* MOLLY *stops her.*)

MOLLY: No! You don't count!

ANNA: That's even worse!

MOLLY: You're on my side!

ANNA: And what gave you that comforting idea?

MOLLY: We sing the same tune, Anna, my dear, just the words are slightly different: me Stephen, you Helmut; me four years, you six; me the Pill, you the miscarriage...

ANNA: We couldn't be further apart...

MOLLY: And suddenly bang goes the drum and the dream is over! Same tune, same drum! That's why we get on so well, Anna, because we don't need them!

ANNA: Really.

MOLLY: Yes, really.

ANNA: No 'really,' I'm sorry to shatter your illusions, but I had lunch with Helmut on Monday, because I still adore him and care about his new marriage to that flat-chested hypochondriac, while you enjoy playing the victim of your own creation, sticking pins into the Stephen doll next to your — may I say — not-exactly-empty bed!

MOLLY: Then why are we celebrating?

ANNA: Certainly not because we don't need them. I think we're doing all this tonight, Molly, old mate, at great expense to salary and self-respect, because we don't have them. Six good tits between us and no man to share them with!

MOLLY: Speak for yourself! I'm fine!

ANNA: It should be my brother's birthday today.

(*Pause*.)

MOLLY: Don't think about it. Try and enjoy yourself for a change.

ANNA: I miss him terribly and I'm raw inside, Molly.

MOLLY: I don't want to think about it. It's just too depressing. Want some pâté?

(*She opens the fridge and looks for the pâté, listening.*)

ANNA: He's a man — or he was a boy-man — and I love him and need him and I want to think about him, so don't tell me to enjoy myself because I'd rather be with him right now than anything in the world, but he's dead! And bang went that dream and that's why I'm here, dressed up like a circus creature, because I'm raw inside and a bit of your salt might help me remember.

(*The phone rings.* ANNA *picks it up.*)

Hello, Solly's Kosher Butchery? No, it's not Molly, who's that? John? (*Covers mouthpiece*) It's John.

MOLLY: *Mazeltov.*

ANNA: Are you home?

MOLLY: No.

ANNA: She's not home.

MOLLY: John who?

ANNA: John who? (*To* MOLLY) Andrew's friend.

MOLLY: Oh. (*Pause.*) Andrew who?

ANNA: Andrew who?

MOLLY: Oh, give me that phone! Yes? John who? Who the hell are you? Who's Andrew? I don't know any Andrew! Of course I'm not home, schmuck, this is a recording! (*Slams down the phone*) Pig!

ANNA: What did you do that for?

MOLLY: What do they think this is? Old Sarah's Whorehouse Special Discount Offer? John who? Andrew who? *Se gat!*

ANNA: Listen, you pretend you can't even understand Afrikaans. So you don't have the right to use vivid phrases like *Se gat* because I know you don't even enjoy saying them. Rather lash out with your own Polack–Anglo-Saxon–Yiddish showstoppers!

MOLLY: Oh, touchy-touchy! You'd really make someone a wonderful friend. What happened to you today, besides the family horror story, which I must admit is a bit gruesome ...

ANNA: Then shut up!

MOLLY: No! This is *my* house, *my* life! I've also been through the mill and dug the grave and smelt the flowers and patted the wreaths, so don't try your anything-you-can-suffer-I-can-bear-better on me. What am I supposed to say? I said it when it happened: I'm sorry your little brother is dead. OK? I didn't create the situation that demanded his blood! It's not my fault!

ANNA: He died protecting your comforts!

MOLLY: Rubbish! He died because that's what happens to soldiers in real life. They don't sell washing-powder; they die!

ANNA: I didn't mean it was your fault ...

MOLLY: Fine. Then don't blame me for your pain, you uptight bitch! It's going to be a happy night tonight and we're all going to suffer our defeats gladly. Do you understand, Anna, old Boer? A 'lovely time'! So tuck away your open wound and smile. You're with someone who's also been there. (*Pause.*) Andrew? Andrew! Oh no, he's the guy with the boat! Did he leave a number?

ANNA: What?

MOLLY: Andrew ... no, who did you speak to?

ANNA: A John.

MOLLY: John! Did he leave a phone number? He invited me for a sail tomorrow. Oh shit, what am I going to do?

ANNA: Try going to church tomorrow.

MOLLY: I went yesterday!

(*She looks through her phone book for the number.*)

ANNA: Let's pick Mouse up on the way. Come on, Molly! Tomorrow will sort itself out.

MOLLY: I've been looking forward to that sail.

ANNA: You've also supposedly been looking forward to tonight.

MOLLY: Tonight's nearly over; I want something nice to look forward to. (*Reads*) A... A... Andrew? Here's Adrian, Avril ... oh, she's emigrated, goodbye Avril. (*Scratches it out*) Ackermann, Abe the chemist, Abe the broker, Abe the lawyer ... no Andrew!

ANNA: Hang around the yacht basin tomorrow, Molly, someone nice is bound to notice you.

MOLLY: That little bastard didn't even give me his surname. Anyway, who can afford a yacht at his age, rich little pig! Let me tell you, a nice long session in the Army would do him a lot of good. Teach him manners for one!

ANNA: Do we have to bring our own wine?

MOLLY: Of course, it's because educated brats like him try to dodge conscription and run and hide overseas that those who enjoy killing children have a free hand!

ANNA: Who can enjoy killing children?

MOLLY: You're asking me? It's because you lot are so desperately clinging to your master-race status that kids are being killed for nothing!

ANNA: My brother was not killed for nothing.

MOLLY: Oh? So what's changed since his pointless death? Nothing has changed; in fact, it's got worse.

ANNA: Do you mean this morning?

MOLLY: The riot in town! And you're supposed to be part of the media?

ANNA: There were twenty-six people killed today.

MOLLY: No, no, darling, don't exaggerate...

ANNA: I saw the telex. I saw the rewritten news bulletin. I read it.

MOLLY: Why aren't we being told?

ANNA: Told what? That we're fighting for our survival?

MOLLY: Your survival, Boer. Mine I fight for all the time. It's part of my heritage. At least I know the day I fall it won't have been for nothing.

ANNA: You're so right, Molly. As an unclaimed corpse you'll look half your age and have the best manicured nails in the morgue.

MOLLY: You're really at your best when you're in a corner.

ANNA: Some survival!

MOLLY: Frankly, old Boer, you lot deserve everything you get. You all need something radical to kick you out of your supremist sleepwalk. And I think a little senseless death in the family is a good beginning . . . Ow!

(ANNA *grabs* MOLLY. *There is a physical scuffle; it must look violent and shocking, nearly masculine. When it is suddenly over, a pause. Both gasp for breath. Eventually* MOLLY *speaks.*)

MOLLY: Jesus . . . what was all that about . . . ?

(*The phone rings.*)

I was only joking . . . you mucked up my hair, you butch bitch . . .

ANNA: I'm sorry . . .

MOLLY: Oh, fuck off, will you, FUCK OFF!!!

(*Pause. The phone rings again.*)

Well, answer the phone! If it's John or whatshisname, say I'm in the bath; take a number . . . be nice to him . . .

(ANNA *picks up the phone.*)

ANNA: Yes? Mouse? Hang on, speak slowly . . . Are you all right? We can pick you up . . . OK. Tell them to drop you here . . . (*Puts down the phone.*) That was Mouse. Her room was burgled.

MOLLY: What?

ANNA: She's on her way. The police will drop her here.

MOLLY: You see, you can't move without people invading your space, stealing all the useless rubbish you can't breathe without!

ANNA: Molly, no one's dead!

MOLLY: It's all so much easier now. Nothing can keep them out. No burglar-bars, no alarms, no guns . . .

ANNA: She called the police . . .

MOLLY: Youth is a burglar. Money . . . beauty . . . hope. All burglars, who creep in so quietly you don't hear them till they

laugh at you and leave you lying for dead ...
(*Pause.*)

ANNA: Did I hurt you?

MOLLY: Not as much as I hope I hurt you. I'm going to phone the police.

ANNA: Mouse has done that.

MOLLY: Please! You know what Mouse is like: stand on her foot and she says 'I'm sorry'. I know a nice young constable in Simonstown.

ANNA: Which is about as useful as a millionaire on the moon. Let's wait till she gets here.

MOLLY: But this is an important night! Things mustn't happen tonight! Not tonight! (*She dials.*) No little burglary is going to lose me that table. You know it's the 'in' place. Everyone tries to get a table ... Hello, Emilio, darling? It's Molly. Hey? *Franco, amore mio* – Molly. Molly, you foreign fart, yes, Anna's friend! You know the old witch with the wart on her nose? Yes? What do you mean 'yes', you schmuck! Listen, Mussolini, I've got contacts in high places. '*Si, signorina*' you can bet your cannelloni! I'll have your work permit revoked, your restaurant declared black, your food branded non-kosher. You'll starve and I'll laugh: HA, HA, HA! Suddenly you remember me? No, I'm fine, considering the world ended ten minutes ago. Listen, Mario, I booked a special table near the window for three at 8.30. Keep it, we're on our way. I know it's your busy night, Mario, but I'm one of your best customers ... but ... but we won't be long ... I promise ... (*To* ANNA, *pleading*) The fucker won't keep our table ... what do I do?

(ANNA *takes the phone and speaks in fluent Italian.*)

ANNA:* *Pronto, Luciano? Anna. Bene, grazie. Siamo un po' in ritardo nell'uscire. Si, Molly è qui e sa la cretina come al solito. Tienimi il tavolo, mi raccomando. Per favore...? Luciano, sei un tesoro!*

---

* Hello, Luciano? Anna. Fine. We're having a bit of a delay in getting away. Yes, Molly's running around like an idiot as usual. Keep the table. For me? Luciano, you're an angel! Keep me some of your *calamares*! Bye!

Mettimi da parte un po' dei tuoi calamari. Ciao! (She puts down the phone casually.) They'll keep our table.

MOLLY: When did you learn to speak Italian?

ANNA: I was bored one Saturday afternoon. Are you all right?

MOLLY: I'm fine. A bit battered round the ego, but that's nothing new.

ANNA: You really still have the habit of bringing out the savages in the best people.

MOLLY: Funny, other people would call it a 'scintillating personality'. Don't rub it in . . .

ANNA: I'm going to watch TV. I need a Valium for my conscience.

MOLLY: No, Anna, don't leave me . . . just sit. Please.

(ANNA *sits. Lights a cigarette. Pause.*)
It's funny.

ANNA: Funny?

MOLLY: Oh yes, funny: bringing out the savages in the best people. I do, you're right. I even get a whiff of their socks from here while I sip my health coffee, knowing I should put that special cream on my face as an investment for the future. Beauty Queen of the Morgue? But I can't, knowing they're twenty and having to pretend in the dark under them that I am too.

ANNA: So fill the tomb with happy laughter, Miss Molly.

MOLLY: Then I pick up my little phone and speak for hours to my other savages, who don't even listen any more, because it's just Molly yakking away. And do you know what's really funny, Anna? I know it. I know they've just put the phone down next to the pot and the pipe and I know they're on their motorbikes on their way to the beach and so I don't stop yakking away for an hour, because it makes me feel better.

ANNA: Mmmm. The non-stop Molly Manure.

MOLLY: Is it that bad?

ANNA: Not if you don't listen.

MOLLY: I could demonstrate to you now. Pick up phone . . . dial . . . dial . . . wait . . . ring, ring, ring: 'Hello, someone, this is Molly!' *Help!!!* (*Pause.*) Too quick. They need at least an hour to register my name, recognize my voice: 'Molly? Molly who? Oh, *that* Molly. It's Molly – pass the coke . . .' (*She looks at* ANNA *with a smile.*) Don't you think that's funny?

ANNA: Hysterically funny.

MOLLY: Funny. Did I tell you about the pain I get here, over my heart?

ANNA: Your heart's on the other side.

MOLLY: No, I think it moved. Agony tore it loose from its moorings. I really think I'm going to die soon.

ANNA: Shall I phone and cancel the table?

MOLLY: Maybe not quite yet, but soon – soon. And what would I have left behind?

ANNA: The echo of a noise.

(*Pause.*)

MOLLY: Is that what you think?

(MOUSE *enters, fraught.*)

MOUSE: Anna! They're writing a ticket for your car!

ANNA: Who?

MOUSE: They say you're illegally parked on the pavement or something.

ANNA: If these damn streets were wider, there'd be no reason to park on the sidewalk. Oh shit!

(*She exits.*)

MOUSE: But it's night! Why do they do things like this at night?

MOLLY: Since when do the police give tickets?

MOUSE: No, traffic police came to me. The real police are too busy. (*She looks around and says* sotto voce) They say they had a complaint.

MOLLY: Bet you it came from those *drekkie* neighbours of mine. It's the woman. She once called the police because I had a party here and didn't invite her. I know what I'll do! I'll make her so terrified she'll be on the next plane to Perth!

(*She starts dialling.*)

MOUSE: You know the number?

MOLLY: That dishy Canadian hippy used to live there with that feather-brained actress with the fat arse, remember? No, before your time . . . it's ringing . . . come on, you fascists, answer! (*The woman answers;* MOLLY *whispers delightedly.*) It's her! (MOLLY *starts breathing heavily*.) Ahhhhhhhh haaaaaaa ahhhhhhhhh ... (*Then stops, quite taken aback*) She laughed and hung up! The bitch! You know, I think it actually turned her on ... what's wrong with you now?

(MOUSE *is laughing with suppressed hysteria*.)

MOUSE: You're mad ... who's going to be frightened of that?

MOLLY: Don't make light of heavy breathers. They're a menace.

MOUSE: You should've said: 'We're going to put a burning tyre round your neck and have a barbecue with your brains!'

(*She cries with laughter*.)

MOLLY: God, that's disgusting ...

(*It just makes* MOUSE *laugh even more. She stumbles out hysterical and passes* ANNA *entering*.)

ANNA: Is she sick?

MOLLY: Sick? That's an understatement!

ANNA: God, don't they have anything better to do!

MOLLY: What happened?

ANNA: I was nice to him.

MOLLY: Afrikaans cop?

ANNA: Of course. The best of them are.

MOLLY: Mouse! For heaven's sake, are we never going to get out of this place?

(ANNA *pours wine*.)

Oh shit, look at my hair ... one would never believe I spent two hours at the hairdresser's this morning. Wonder if I should cut it? (*She fiddles with her hair*.) What do you think? Short-short? Or maybe change the colour?

ANNA: Leave colour out of this, just for tonight.

MOLLY: And what's wrong with you now!

ANNA: I'm hungry!

MOLLY: I hate it when you go all uptight and Afrikaans and unreasonable.

ANNA: Unreasonable? I just want some food and wine – not a black eye, or a parking ticket, or to apologize because I exist!

MOLLY: You've already had enough wine.

ANNA: So what did Mouse say about the burglary?

MOLLY: And don't change the subject! Even if you don't like it, I

still have the right to say certain things to you. That's what good friends are for.
ANNA: You'll make someone a wonderful friend, Molly.
MOLLY: And I'm sober. And you're fairly sober, for a change. So cool it on the booze tonight.
ANNA: I'm just sipping little bits to keep sane.
MOLLY: If you're tense, take Valium like a normal person. You 'sip' too much! You always get pissed and become loud and political and embarrassing.
ANNA: Oh, make a phone-call, Molly. I don't need the Ten Commandments from you.
MOLLY: We at least own the copyright! You drink too much!
ANNA: I wonder what's really happening out there...
(*She opens the kitchen door and looks out.*)
MOLLY: I know, because I don't drink and I watch you fall to pieces and I worry, because I love you and care for you.
ANNA: Careful, I'll cry.
MOLLY: You'll have an accident one night in your big fast car, and you'll be dead, Anna, just because you're so full of cheap wine, you won't even notice your head come off!
ANNA: It's so quiet out there you can hear the angels of death beating their wings in time to the requiem...
MOLLY: Talk about it, damn it!
ANNA: Talk about what?
MOLLY: Don't be so cool and monumental!
ANNA: Talk about what?
MOLLY: Crack a bit, Anna, it's all in the family!
(*Pause.*)
ANNA: I don't want to talk about my love for ... God, who? Helmut? My brother?
MOLLY: Me?
ANNA: Loathing for you? Maybe. For me, definitely. Pick your card.
MOLLY: See, hairy round the gills, woof, woof, woof!
ANNA: I don't find any of this funny.
MOLLY: No, you Afrikaners have got a wonderful sense of humour, but only when you're amused! You can't bear to take a

friendly word of warning ... forget criticism. I mean, who am I to criticize you? One chosen people doesn't criticize another chosen people! (*Pause.*) I care, Anna. I worry. You lie to me.

ANNA: I tell you nothing.

MOLLY: Exactly. You all pretend nothing's wrong – nothing's wrong – nothing's wrong – nothing's wrong ...

ANNA: No sirens ... no shots ... no screams ... no nothing ... (*She listens outside.*)

MOLLY: You're lonely, I'm lonely – I don't lie, I rub it in! You're getting old, I'm getting old – I don't lie, I rub it out! I bitch about the cost and pay the bill, but I don't lie! You're so desperate to be accepted, Anna, you'll soon just be that charmless bodiless voice on the radio, giving false truth to even more lies. You're a professional liar!

ANNA: I'm an Afrikaner.

MOLLY: Once in our lives together ... we laughed a lot, you remember, Anna?

ANNA: Long ago.

MOLLY: We laughed at each other, with each other.

ANNA: Did we?

MOLLY: Why don't we notice those things any more, Anna?

ANNA: Because those things just aren't funny any more.

MOLLY: No. But other people still laugh. Something must be funny somewhere, mustn't it?

ANNA: It's all crazy ...

MOLLY: Must we also first go mad to be able to laugh again?

(MOUSE *enters, crying.*)

Ah ha! No more sick little jokes about disgusting things? Like my grandmother always said in Poland: '*Mein Kind*, after the big laugh always comes a bigger tear!'

MOUSE: They took everything I'd saved ...

ANNA: Money? You didn't keep it in a bank?

MOUSE: Someone said the bank might collapse, so I took it all out last week and hid it in my room ...

MOLLY: I don't believe it! Where did you hide it?

MOUSE: The mattress ...

MOLLY: You should've hidden it in your underwear. No one would've looked there.
ANNA: Is your passport safe?
> (MOUSE *nods and holds it up.* ANNA *takes it from her and goes to the drawer in the sideboard where William went earlier. She opens it and puts the passport in. Stares into the drawer.* MOLLY *goes on regardless.*)

MOLLY: My grandmother knew the writing on the wall when she saw it. She'd laugh today, let me tell you.
ANNA: Molly, do you keep a gun?
MOLLY: What?
ANNA: A gun.
MOLLY: Next to my bed, why?
> (ANNA *shakes her head and closes the drawer slowly.*)

My grandmother was an incredible person, let me tell you. Of course, I never knew her. She was killed by the Nazis. My father's cousin was murdered by the SS. My father's oldest sister was massacred by the Russians. My second cousin on my mother's side was accidentally executed by the Americans. My relatives have in turn been killed by everyone, and here I am. Molly. Molly Mashuga with, as her best friends, a Boer and a shikse. Where? The southern tip of nowhere. Why? Because it's heaven and it's mine and I love it! They took everything?
MOUSE: Hey? Oh yes: my shampoo, the suitcase, which was real leather, the alarm clock, those shoes I got last month . . .
MOLLY: Yes, yes, yes, well, go and find something in my room. We must go now!
MOUSE: I don't think I want to . . .
ANNA: What did the police say?
MOUSE: They suspect a coloured gang. They say that this afternoon the riot squads chased a whole lot of coloured rioters up into this area. It's all political, you know, Anna. If I'd been there, I'm sure they would have killed me.
MOLLY: Yes: put a tyre round your neck and barbecued your brains?
MOUSE: I'm sorry I said that . . .

ANNA: Any tuppence-ha'penny crook can now throw a petrol-bomb at an old white lady and become an international hero.
MOUSE: The traffic cop said that it was political unrest and was I insured for riot cover.
MOLLY: Are you?
MOUSE: Riot cover? I don't know ...
(MOLLY *picks up the phone*.)
MOLLY: What was that policeman's name, the one you spoke to?
MOUSE: He was a traffic cop.
MOLLY: No, you said the police spoke to you as well?
MOUSE: The traffic cop phoned the police, yes.
MOLLY: Where was he stationed?
MOUSE: I don't know.
MOLLY: What do you mean you don't know! Are you insured or aren't you insured?
MOUSE: I don't know.
MOLLY: You don't know. Didn't I say let my broker handle your affairs? Didn't I say give me your money to invest on an on-call basis at 22 per cent?
MOUSE: I didn't want to be a burden, Molly. I'm old enough to handle my own affairs.
MOLLY: Handle your own affairs? You've got no damn affairs left to handle! At least with me they would have been in good hands.
ANNA: A debatable point.
MOLLY: And you stay out of this. What are you doing that's so constructive? Mouse, how did they get in?
MOUSE: I don't know ...
MOLLY: Ask a silly question ... (*She dials angrily*.) I hate being forced to use my contacts, but I will, seeing as you haven't a clue how to sort this nonsense out. Dear God ... Hello, Simonstown Police? Listen, my dear, can I speak to Constable Green? Yes, it's very important. (*Glares at* MOUSE) You don't know. If you live like a punk, this is what you should expect!
MOUSE: (*Sobs*) I'm not living like a punk ...
MOLLY: Shhhh. Hello, darling, it's Molly. We've just had a terrible burglary down the road and, my dear, we know it's these

coloured kids and they're all over the place and . . . Oh. OK, I'll hang on. (*Pause*.) He told me to hang on. What's the time?

ANNA: We've lost the table.

MOLLY: For God's sake, Mouse, go into my dressing-room and find something decent to wear. You can't go dressed like a . . . a . . .

ANNA: A punk.

MOUSE: Anna, I don't want to go . . .

MOLLY: You're all making too much noise, I can't hear a word. Hello? Yes? I'm holding on for Constable Green, he knows me as a friend . . . of course it's urgent! All hell's broken loose up here! OK, OK, I'll wait. (*She sighs and waits*.) Mouse, there's a nice kaftan thing I got from those promotion crooks, who still owe me a fortune, by the way. (*Into phone*) Yes, I'm still here . . . what's happening in Simonstown, for God's sake? The Russian invasion? Mouse, don't sit there like a Muppet, help me make this night a success. At the moment it's death – *death!* (*Suddenly into phone*) No, no, no one's dead, we've just had a burglary. Yes, we've seen some traffic cop from town . . . well, it's a long story, the police were busy . . . I know you're busy . . . this girl has lost all her documents. A fortune in jewellery! Listen, you rude little man, what do I pay taxes for? Oh, but . . . yes . . . OK, OK, bye. (*She puts down the phone*.) He says they're busy. In Simonstown?

ANNA: Nice friends and contacts you have.

MOLLY: Constable Green has been transferred, OK?

MOUSE: Everyone's on permanent stand-by under the State of Emergency, the cop said. He said things are bad.

MOLLY: Jesus, Simonstown? What the hell could be happening there that's more important?

MOUSE: Molly? Anna? I'm sorry, I just can't face a party tonight . . . really . . .

ANNA: We quite understand, Mousie . . .

MOLLY: Rubbish! You're both being menstrual about tonight. Tonight has been booked for weeks.

MOUSE: But . . .

MOLLY: Tonight is Christmas! Tonight is Easter! Tonight is the end of the world!

ANNA: And we're going to have a party?

MOLLY: You're damn right! So get your arse in there and find yourself a suitable skin and smile!
(MOLLY *pushes* MOUSE *out of the room.*)
Some help you've been.
ANNA: But I'm a useless alcoholic, remember?
MOLLY: Don't tempt the devil . . .
(*A knock on the kitchen door.*)
Now what the hell is this? (*Shouts*) No, thank you, I've already given!
(*The kitchen door opens and* WILLIAM *appears tentatively.*)
WILLIAM: Evening. You must be Molly?
MOLLY: Hey?
ANNA: Cover your ears, Anna?
WILLIAM: I've . . . er . . . I've come for my bag.
MOLLY: Anna, it's for you.
ANNA: Just whistle when you've finished!
(*She jauntily exits with a wink at* WILLIAM.)
MOLLY: Wait, Anna, damn it . . . look, you've got the wrong house. Does this look like a brothel? Don't answer . . .
WILLIAM: I wouldn't know the answer.
MOLLY: Oh? Quick too? What do you want? I'm on my way out.
WILLIAM: You don't remember me, then?
MOLLY: Should I?
WILLIAM: No, it was some years ago.
MOLLY: What was some years ago?
WILLIAM: I was here.
MOLLY: Ah well, since then I've had a few other boys in to fix the house. Plumbers, painters, carpenters, carpeters, TV men, hi-fi men, mechanics, electricians . . .
WILLIAM: And a plasterer that ripped you off. (*He indicates the crack in the wall.*) You hadn't done all this when I was here last. I've always wanted to come up and have a look, but I've never had the chance, you know.
MOLLY: Fancy that.
WILLIAM: Yes. Who's next door?
MOLLY: Pigs. Want a job there?
WILLIAM: Does the crack go through to their side?

MOLLY: The thought keeps me awake *all* night, but you must forgive me, I have to drag myself away now, I'm so sorry.

WILLIAM: You got a message from Mrs Peters?

MOLLY: Mrs Peters?

WILLIAM: She was hurt. I can't get through to her house. The phones must be down.

MOLLY: You're not looking for a job?

WILLIAM: On a Saturday night?

MOLLY: I don't put anything past you people.

WILLIAM: Us coloureds you mean?

MOLLY: I have got nothing against coloureds! Some of my best friends . . .

WILLIAM: Are blacks?

MOLLY: Some of my best friends have black friends. Well, if you're such an intimate friend of Mrs Peters, tell her I need her here on Monday morning.

WILLIAM: She gets up at four o'clock to be here at seven.

MOLLY: That's what she gets paid for. I have an important luncheon on the patio and it looks a mess!

WILLIAM: Just needs a sweep with a good broom.

MOLLY: You seem to know a lot about my house.

WILLIAM: No. Not everything. (*Pause. He is very charming.*) What's through there?

MOLLY: Various rooms.

WILLIAM: Including your bedroom?

MOLLY: Yes.

WILLIAM: Ah.

MOLLY: Where I sleep.

WILLIAM: Ah.

MOLLY: Very exotic, very seductive – no windows, teak coffin on crushed red velvet, you know, the very latest design. I keep a Coke bottle filled with the best blood at body temperature. Wonderful for hangovers!

WILLIAM: You're funny.

MOLLY: And you're a wonderful audience. It's just that we're on our way out. Maybe you can pop in some other time?

WILLIAM: You want to offer me a job?

MOLLY: Depends what you do best. (*Pause*.) And next time come to the front door. I am not ashamed of receiving coloureds.
WILLIAM: Gosh, thanks, hey. (*He goes to the door*.) Is this all the security you have on the door?
(*He fingers the chain*.)
MOLLY: Yes...
WILLIAM: No good. OK, bye.
MOLLY: No, wait a minute...
WILLIAM: Oh, by the way, thanks for keeping Rambo locked up.
(*He exits, smiling*.)
MOLLY: Rambo? What the hell is going on here!
(ANNA *enters*.)
ANNA: What did he want?
MOLLY: My hand in marriage. I just had this chain put on last month!
ANNA: I can't make it a late night. I have to prepare my programme tomorrow; we record on Monday.
MOLLY: Jesus Christ!
ANNA: What is it?
MOLLY: That little fucker! Do you know, I think he was planning to rob me?
ANNA: Oh, come on!
MOLLY: No, he was taking a chance, first trying the door and then giving me all that spiel about Mrs Peters.
ANNA: I wouldn't worry, if he knows Mrs Peters.
MOLLY: That little bastard would have walked into my house and just helped himself to all my things! Like they've done to Mouse!
ANNA: Nonsense, we're all here.
MOLLY: So? He'd bang us on the head and rob and rape and plunder...
ANNA: Wishful thinking.
MOLLY: Damn this country!
ANNA: You've got your gun, Molly...
(*She takes the gun out of the drawer and looks at it*.)
MOLLY: Let me see that.
ANNA: It's loaded... no, it's been used... when did you shoot with it?
MOLLY: It's not mine. (*She takes it and studies it*.) I think it belongs to one of the twins. They always come to bed with their guns

strapped to their thighs. Very confusing.

ANNA: I can imagine. Why have the twins got guns, for goodness' sake?

MOLLY: Why does the sun rise?

ANNA: I'm not going to hang around to watch it.

MOLLY: Don't bellow, I heard you.
>   (*She puts the gun back in the drawer.*)

ANNA: Frankly, I don't feel like it.

MOLLY: You don't feel like it?

ANNA: No, I'd much rather go home.

MOLLY: Really? You'd rather go home.

ANNA: Yes, frankly.

MOLLY: Yes, very frank. And Mouse?

ANNA: I think she should come and spend the weekend with me at home.

MOLLY: Oh, how cosy. And what about me?

ANNA: Hey?

MOLLY: Don't 'hey' me – hay is what horses eat! What about me?

ANNA: Molly . . .

MOLLY: I want to go out, I need to go out . . .

ANNA: Molly . . .

MOLLY: Right! Molly! Molly! Molly exists!

ANNA: OK, just not too late!

MOLLY: Molly exists!

ANNA: All right!

MOLLY: *Molly exists!*

ANNA: You've got lipstick on your teeth.
>   (MOLLY *drops the dramatics.*)

MOLLY: Oh shit. I'm so sick of all this camouflage. When will the world accept me, warts and all? Now where's that f— unmentionable Mouse. MOUSE!!!
>   (MOUSE *enters in a kaftan.*)

MOUSE: I feel like an Arab.

MOLLY: Well, you won't find one in this house.

ANNA: (*Laughs*) Good God, Mouse . . .

MOLLY: I'm just getting my lipstick. Now, no one move. I have this terrible feeling you'll both run away and leave me to face it on my own. It's got to be a happy night! I can't do it on my own!

(*She exits.* MOUSE *self-consciously sits.*)

ANNA: You look amazing.

MOUSE: Really?

ANNA: Quite indescribable.

MOUSE: Thanks.

ANNA: They really took everything?

MOUSE: My writing-paper, my perfume, my spare pair of glasses...

ANNA: You OK?

MOUSE: Oh yes. I'm not as attached to things as you and Molly.

ANNA: That only happens when you can afford it. (*She pours some more wine.*) Cheers.

(MOLLY *enters, ready to go.*)

MOLLY: Come on, come on, we're terribly late! Fridge closed, door locked, chain on... fucking useless chain! Stove off, oven off, phone off... (*Takes the phone off the hook*) Will you two bitches get out of here? We'll lose the table. Mouse, is the joint licensed?

MOUSE: I don't know.

MOLLY: You don't know. Who knows?

ANNA: No, it's not.

MOLLY: Bring the red wine.

ANNA: It's in my tummy.

MOLLY: All of it! Alcoholic bitch!

MOUSE: There's some white in the fridge.

MOLLY: It gives me pimples...

(ANNA *sighs dangerously.*)

But don't worry, girls, I've found a cure. I shall wear a mask! (*Takes white wine out of the fridge*) Now, have you done everything? Yes. I'll leave suicide for later. Cheer up, my friends, the night is but a teenager! (*Picks up Anna's glass*) What's this waste?

ANNA: Dregs.

MOLLY: Very suitable. I drink to three of the nicest girls I know. *Lachaim!* (*She drains the glass and pulls a face.*) Ugh! And now let's go and kick the world up its arse!

(*Blackout.*)

END OF ACT ONE

Act Two

———————o———————

Later. ANNA *and* MOUSE, *still dressed up, are sitting at the kitchen table.* ANNA *is drinking wine.*

ANNA: Is this her idea of a joke?
MOUSE: They say the road-blocks are for our own protection, Anna.
ANNA: So now one can't even move about one's own city?
MOUSE: I still think we would've got into that nice Indian place.
ANNA: What are people doing in expensive restaurants, feasting and boozing and having such a good time in the middle of a revolution?
MOUSE: She's going to blame me.
ANNA: It's disgusting.
MOUSE: I can't help being burgled.
ANNA: They seem to have been celebrating something.
MOUSE: It is Saturday night.

(ANNA *looks around the kitchen.*)

ANNA: Has anyone ever told Molly what a ghastly place this is?
MOUSE: It won a prize.
ANNA: How much does she pay for the honour? R1,000 a month?
MOUSE: That's what you paid for that dress.
ANNA: No one was thrown out of this dress to make room for me!
MOUSE: I want to go home.
ANNA: What home? You don't have a home!

(MOLLY *enters. She has changed into casual clothes.*)

MOLLY: So we lost the table. It's not the end of the world. We'll just never go there again. Never!
ANNA: I knew this would happen.
MOLLY: Oh, my clairvoyant friend! If you had any real clout you could've talked those police into letting us through the road-block and not wasting an hour breathing in exhaust-fumes!

ANNA: I said don't take the main road . . .

MOLLY: Yes, yes, blame Molly for everything. You two have been enough of a pain in the arse all night, so I'll be relieved to take the blame for my party. Well, sit down and shut up, we've only just started. Who's got money?

MOUSE: They took all my . . .

MOLLY: I've only got my chequebook and the plastic. Come on, who's got real money?

ANNA: In my bag.

MOLLY: I'll get us some Chinese takeaways. We all love Chinese food, don't we?

(*No reaction.*)

Thought so. And you don't have to look so murderous, Anna old Boer. You're stuck with me, so make the best of an occasion. And don't either of you move! I'll be back before the blacks take over!

(*She exits. Pause.* ANNA *pours more wine.*)

ANNA: Want some?

MOUSE: No.

ANNA: What do you want?

MOUSE: I'm not thirsty.

ANNA: What do you want, Mouse!

MOUSE: You mean from life? A man. A child. Feeling safe. Like you.

ANNA: Oh no.

MOUSE: No?

ANNA: I want everything. Man–child–safety is just a consolation prize. I want everything.

MOUSE: At any cost.

ANNA: Yes.

MOUSE: I don't like you

ANNA: Nor do I. Can't you wear a belt or something? You look pregnant.

MOUSE: Don't worry, I'm not. (*Giggles*) I've been robbed, not raped!

(ANNA *ignores her little joke. The phone rings.*)

ANNA: How come Molly's always alone if that phone never stops ringing? Maybe she's phoning herself from the corner phone-box just to impress us.

MOUSE: Shouldn't we answer it?

ANNA: You answer it. You've made a career out of taking messages.

MOUSE: I'm not on switchboard any more, Anna. I now take the scenic tours.

ANNA: Sorry.

(MOUSE *answers the phone*.)

MOUSE: Hello? 443 0809? No, she's not here. Yes, hold on, please. Anna, it's for you.

(ANNA *takes the phone*.)

ANNA: Suicides Unanimous? Oh, Mommie? No, I'm OK, Mommie. No, I'm not drunk! Just me and Molly and the Mouse. We went out to a steakhouse ... it's a long story. I thought we'd discussed all this, Mommie. It's my night off! Auntie Sybil is there with you? Yes, I know it's his birthday and I should be there, but I'm not there, I'm here; so please – leave me alone! (*She puts down the phone*.) It's my brother's birthday today.

MOUSE: Oh.

ANNA: Yes.

MOUSE: I'm sorry.

ANNA: Why?

MOUSE: He's dead. Birthdays are different when you're dead.

ANNA: Oh yes? He can do nothing wrong now, never. He's safe and dead and always like the picture in the frame. While Anna stumbles through life black and blue and pathetically alive. (*Pause*.) I want nothing more than anyone else. Is that asking for so much? And when I drive around town after midnight, looking at all the young men and brown men and gay men ... any men ... I always end up driving home alone and I ask myself: 'Why Anna? What's wrong with you, Anna? Why don't you have someone to love you, like everyone else?' That's all I want, Mousie. I want the impossible, the ordinary. We're not ordinary, you know? You and me and Molly? We're three of the last Great White Blind ... Losers! Here, now, with what's falling apart around us, so does it really matter if you pretend you're deaf as well? With your head up your own arse you can dance for a long time before you hear them laughing at you. (*She sings drunkenly and dances around the kitchen. She stops, regains her balance and takes out a cigarette.*) Matches.

(MOUSE *hands her some matches.*)

Hey, where's that expensive Dunhill lighter I gave you for your birthday? Have you pawned it?

MOUSE: It was stolen with my jewellery box in which I kept special things. How can you think I would pawn it!

ANNA: You're supposed to use a lighter, Mouse.

MOUSE: I don't smoke.

ANNA: Oh. What's the time?

MOUSE: Late.

ANNA: So they even took that lighter? It cost a fortune!

MOUSE: I'm sorry, Anna.

ANNA: People shouldn't steal.

MOUSE: Maybe they needed my things more than I did.

ANNA: You're going to become a nun!

MOUSE: No. What really scares me is that someone can so easily get into my privacy without me knowing.

ANNA: Yes; now go and telex Daddykins for a cheque.

MOUSE: That's not nice, Anna.

ANNA: But I'm not a 'Nice Anna'.

MOUSE: I've never run to my father for help!

ANNA: Then you're a fool.

MOUSE: I don't think so.

(*Pause.*)

ANNA: I'm going.

MOUSE: Anna, you can't drive in your state.

ANNA: I'm sick of all this crap. I feel like a fool, sitting around here talking rubbish to you. Tell Molly our house was burnt down by terrorists or something. (*She gets up and sways to the door. Stops, confused*) I better take the gun . . .

MOUSE: Where are you going?

ANNA: I don't know . . . maybe I've been invited to someone's house . . . yes, I've just remembered. A nice young man, slightly older than me. He has prospects and manners and money. He can talk about all sorts of things, like me and my work and my life: the ultimate man. I'm going to meet him now. I said I'd come anyway, because I knew tonight would be a flop!

MOUSE: Let me come with you?

ANNA: Where to?

MOUSE: Do you think I'm enjoying myself?

ANNA: Oh, yes, we're all suffering and we love it!

MOUSE: Please let's go somewhere where we can talk.

ANNA: I don't want to talk to you, Mouse.

MOUSE: Oh.

ANNA: You're a neurotic. You get burgled. You'll probably get murdered one day. You have no secrets, no success, no opinions. You're a sponge, a drain on the brain. And you're not even pretty. And about as sexy as a freeway road-sign. I'd rather talk to myself.

MOUSE: You couldn't mean that...

ANNA: Or to one of the empty-headed studs I pick up at the discos. At least that 'Want a spin in my new Mercedes?' sometimes leads to something. I can't sleep with you. I can't love you.

MOUSE: You've never tried to love me.

ANNA: You're just not my type, little Mouse. Wild lesbian passion just doesn't happen among our master race. We're all as pure as the driven shit!

MOUSE: You've just had too much to drink and you are saying things you'll regret, Anna.

ANNA: Too late...

(*The phone rings again.*)

Can you believe it? Imagine if they had to bug Molly's phone, they'd never have time to go to the lavatory. Maybe that's a call from Casualty. Some medic with Molly's Japanese pearl necklace between his fingers, still sticky with her blood. Next of kin's not home! Throw Molly on the garbage heap! (*She picks up the phone.*) Yes! (*Puts the phone down quickly*) God, my mother gets on my nerves! OK! OK! I'll stay here till the bitch gets back, all right! But what do I drink? What do I do?

MOUSE: Try dropping dead!
(MOUSE *bursts into tears and exits.* ANNA *goes to the sideboard and opens the drawer in search of the gun. She empties the drawer on to the floor: no gun. We hear* MOLLY's *voice.*)
MOLLY: (*Off*) Party! Party! Pull up your knickers, Mother's home! Enough noodles to kill us all!
(*The phone rings.* MOLLY *enters.*)
Jesus Christ, what's been happening here! Well, answer the bloody phone, for God's sake! What do you think I invited you here for, huh? Dinner? Like hell! Sweet-and-sour pork, chicken chop suey and a nice mushy, slushy vegetarian thing for the rodent. I said answer the phone!
ANNA: Answer the phone yourself!
MOLLY: Oh me, oh my, but we are on good form tonight! What a joy to have around. (*She picks up the drawer and replaces the towels and puts it back into the sideboard.*) Oh, bugger off, Boer, I don't need you! I'm having a wonderful time, so don't piss on my picnic! Go home, go to hell, do anything, just don't sit around my kitchen looking tragically monumental. Self-indulgent cow! OK? (*She picks up the phone and speaks in an Irish accent.*) You've got the wrong number. We're all nuns and we aren't supposed to do that sort of thing! Goodbye! (*Puts down the phone*) Right, you like sweet-and-sour? I've got some spring rolls. (*In Chinese accent*) Spling lolls? If you can't *do* it, you might as well *eat* it! (*Pause.*) God, you smell of death. And cheap wine!
ANNA: Your cheap wine!
MOLLY: Now where the hell is Mouse? Mouse! Don't tell me she's run away, don't tell me!
ANNA: It smells like garbage.
MOLLY: Well it's not garbage, it's Chinese. Unless they also rate as Rubbish in your all-white master-mind? Tell me, who do you lot like? You hate the Jews, the Catholics, the blacks, the yellows, the browns and the reds. There's no one left. You've chased them all away and now you're alone in the cemetery, old Boer, so shut up and eat your chicken soup. Mouse!
(MOUSE *enters in a dressing-gown.*)

About time. I brought you some ... (MOLLY *sees her properly*.) And what the hell do you think you're wearing? This is a formal do!

MOUSE: I don't feel well. Do you have something ...

MOLLY: An abortionist? Easy. Look in my phone book, under A. There's a lovely Mrs Meyer in Mowbray.

(MOUSE *starts crying*.)

Oh, for heavens sake.

ANNA: Jesus God!!!

(*She exits furiously*.)

MOLLY: And don't you blaspheme in my house. Fucking fascist! Now why is everyone behaving like pigs? It's not Christmas!

(*She helps* MOUSE *to sit at the table*.)

OK, Mousie, I'm sorry, I'm also tense. Come now, stop the tears. You'll rust the gold in your chain. What do you want? A pill? Do you have a headache? Mouse? (*She produces a 'medical kit' full of bottles*.) Here. A pill for each season. What's sore? The head? Take one of these ... no, these are for periods – oh, what the hell, same difference. Here's one for ... piles? You know what piles are, Mouse? I thought not. Gastroenteritis ... have you been sick? Oh shit, Mouse, I can smell it – you've been sick! Listen, you didn't vomit all over my bathroom, did you? Mrs Peters isn't coming in till Monday. Know what your problem is? You don't eat properly. Listen to me, I know. What do you expect when you always nibble at leaves like a rabbit – you get sick. If rabbits ate ice-cream, they'd also get sick. It makes total sense! Here's a spring roll. Eat it. Go on, I won't stop yakking till I see you eat properly. Eat the fucking roll, Mouse! It's OK. No meat. I specially asked. There. Nice, hey? Hey? Want some sweet-and-sour ... no. Some of this? Ugh, what is this afterbirth? Oh, the nice vegetarian thing I got specially for you. Specially! Now eat! You'll feel better. (*Pause*.) What went wrong, for God's sake? It was so simple. A little dinner for three. Simple.

MOUSE: Sorry ...

MOLLY: 'Sorry'? And when do I get my chance? You all throw tantrums and bitch and snot and vomit and then say 'Sorry'

and forget about it, but what about me? When do I have my moment? I'm not the perfect saint; I also need to explode.
(MOUSE *can't help laughing at* MOLLY.)
All right, you'll choke to death; rather cut your wrists!
(ANNA *enters quickly.*)
Look who's back! Coming to apologize? I thought being an Afrikaner meant never having to say 'I'm sorry!'
(ANNA *dials a phone number impatiently.*)

ANNA: Is that the police? Lieutenant van Heerden! Yes, it's very important!

MOLLY: What do we need the police for?

ANNA: Hello, Jan? *My kar is gesteel ... Anna. Hier bo in Loaderstraat. Ja, Jan, ek weet dis Saterdagaand in die Kaap. Dis 'n nuwe Mercedes! Maar dis die riot squad se probleem!*[1]

MOLLY: Anna, what's going on?

ANNA: *Nee, Jan, Kom nou! Of sal ek liewers direk vir my Oom bel? Goed.*[2]
(*She puts down the phone.*)

MOLLY: What was all that about?

ANNA: If you're that interested, learn the language!
(*She exits.* MOLLY *follows her off.*)

MOLLY What about the riot squad? Is something happening? Anna!
(MOUSE *is left alone in the kitchen. She waits for a moment, then checks that no one is looking. Then she digs into the sweet-and-sour pork with her fingers and eats with relish.* WILLIAM *enters from the house. He has been there all the time, having got in while they were out. When* MOUSE *sees him, she gets a shock.*)

WILLIAM: Shhhh! Don't say a word!

MOUSE: Don't you say a word either!

WILLIAM: Why?

---

[1] Hello Jan? My car has been stolen ... Anna. Up here in Loader Street. Yes, Jan, I know it's Saturday evening in the Cape. It's a new Mercedes! But it's the riot squad's problem!

[2] No, Jan, come now! Or shall I phone my uncle instead? Good.

MOUSE: I'm eating meat! What's happening in the street?
WILLIAM: It seems your friend's Mercedes was stolen.
MOUSE: You'd better go . . . what are you doing here?
   (*Pause.* MOUSE *gets nervous.*)
WILLIAM: You must believe me. I'm William Peters.
MOUSE: Who?
WILLIAM: Mrs Peters is my mother.
MOUSE: Oh.
WILLIAM: I came this morning. She was working here. I gave her something to keep for me. I just came back for it, that's all.
MOUSE: You were in the house?
WILLIAM: It's OK now. I've got what I came for.
   (*He holds up the bag containing the fruit and vegetables.*)
MOUSE: Were you being chased by the police?
WILLIAM: Just a way of life. Here, don't leave this lying around.
   (*He hands her the passport.* MOUSE *looks at the drawer, then opens it. Gasps*)
MOUSE: The gun! You took the gun!
WILLIAM: It doesn't belong to me . . .
   (ANNA *and* MOLLY *are heard returning.*)
MOUSE: Here they come . . . go away . . . go!
   (*She pushes him to the kitchen door, but the safety chain is on and they can't open it.*)
MOUSE: Oh God, they'll get the police if they find you here. Hide!
WILLIAM: I'll just tell them . . .
MOUSE: Don't be crazy . . . hide!
   (*She pushes him into the small pantry alcove so that he is hidden from the action area but in view of the audience.* ANNA *enters briskly, followed by* MOLLY.)
MOLLY: . . . but, Anna, just locking things doesn't help, I've told you before. It's OK for the insurance, but they get into anything nowadays! Nothing is safe! Now she's blaming me!
ANNA: I'm not blaming you.
MOLLY: You make me feel it's all my fault!
ANNA: My fault for coming here tonight. Shit!
MOUSE: That's a ten-rand fine.
   (*They both look at her amazed. She points to the tin.*)

You said a swear-word. Tin.

MOLLY: Fuck the tin, Mouse! How can I help it? Cars get stolen all the time. It's the coloureds! They steal everything!

MOUSE: Let's go and sit inside?

MOLLY: Who has a car like that anyway? The country's economy has gone down the drain and you lot get bigger cars every month. That's asking for trouble. We whites have become safe targets for blacks, Anna. These kids are like viruses. They'll get into anything they can.

MOUSE: Leave the coloureds out of this.

MOLLY: Hello. And whose side are you on?

MOUSE: I'm sure there's something nice on TV in the lounge ... come.

MOLLY: After what you went through this morning – nearly blinded by tear-gas, nearly blown to bits by bombs, nearly massacred, now you take their side?

MOUSE: It's not always the coloureds who steal ...

MOLLY: So who steals around here? The whites? What for, we've got everything already!

MOUSE: You stole this house from the coloureds.

MOLLY: Oh, don't start on that again! I don't make the laws around here. It's not my fault!

ANNA: Calm down, Molly! Jan said he'd be up here as soon as the pressure is off.

MOLLY: 1999?

MOUSE: Isn't that Jan van Heerden, your friend who took us mountain-climbing that weekend?

ANNA: You quite fancied him?

MOLLY: God! A few petrol-bombs and rioting schoolkids and they call it a revolution! Shame! You should've been in Poland in the ghetto in Warsaw!

ANNA: Well I wasn't.

MOLLY: Obviously. Now it's all cold!

(*She picks at the food angrily.* MOUSE *is very aware of* WILLIAM *hiding and tries to prevent the others from going towards that area.*)

Where are the fucking plates?

MOUSE: I'll get them!
   (*She goes over to where* WILLIAM *is, leans across him and takes the plates one by one.*)
ANNA: But tell us more, Molly.
MOLLY: About what?
ANNA: Your pre-natal Polish connection.
MOLLY: It's too painful. Mouse, what are you doing?
MOUSE: Getting the fucking plates . . .
   (*She gets nervous, giggles and puts the plates on the table.*)
ANNA: Then suffer a bit, Molly. Tell me about the horrors, the atrocities. Was your mother ever raped?
MOLLY: Hey?
ANNA: In the Warsaw ghetto? Raped: by . . . what were they now?
MOUSE: Nazis, Russians, Allies, Americans. Can't we go and eat inside?
MOLLY: Look, it might be a joke to you, but it's my life! I don't need to prove anything! Here's a spring roll.
   (*She throws one at* ANNA *who ducks, and it falls to the floor.*)
MOUSE: Molly, are you going to start throwing food around again?
ANNA: And what about the inhuman suffering, Molly? The Warsaw ghetto overcrowded and stinking? People evicted from their homes and transported to camps of tin shacks and no water or warmth?
MOLLY: So you've read Leon Uris, big deal!
ANNA: No, I've driven our maid to her home a few times.
MOLLY: What are you getting at?
ANNA: Just making odious comparisons. Same tune, same drum; except here you're the one who says: 'But I swear I didn't know what was happening, I swear!'
MOLLY: Mouse, come and eat something before I really start throwing it around!
MOUSE: I'm not hungry.
MOLLY: God, you make me sick! Both of you! You bore me to death.
ANNA: Our national disease! Boredom! The symptoms are all the good things in life without the need to pay for them, in blood.
   (*She opens a new bottle of wine. Her attitude throughout this is*

casual.) I think I also have the sickness. I keep on doing silly, desperate things, like spending time with you to forget, in case I wake up and see my real face reflected in the pools of blood at my feet. It's such 'fun', you see, playing dodge the tear-gas canisters at varsity, but getting safely home in time to watch the replay on TV. Some terminal cases get themselves locked up in detention, thank God, without trial, as an investment for that political asylum and accompanying highly paid international martyrdom ... and then there's us, dying pathetically of boredom. Life we shun because we've forgotten how to live it decently. Rather hide behind our armour – our money, our cars, our investments – because it's the only reality we're left with. The colour of our skin has become our sex and the trappings of superiority our appeal!

MOLLY: Welcome to the Club, Anna!

ANNA: But the death-defying difference between me and you is that me and mine went through it all *here* and stuck to it and won before going rotten, while you and yours went through it somewhere else and lost and ran. But there's still a lot of room left in our *laager*, Molly, if you can bear the smell. So, girls, welcome to the club!

MOLLY: You're drunk!

ANNA: But now that you've both grown rich and fat on the laws of my land, remember that because of me and mine, you two also have a soapbox to stand on, and without me and mine, where would you be? Back in a sandstorm behind barbed wire? And somehow I don't see you taking that last train to Manenberg with smiles on your faces. So cheers, girls! I drink to us and our orange, white and blue heaven. Let's enjoy it while it lasts: very quietly.

(*She laughs and drinks.*)

MOLLY: You are drunk!

(ANNA *is about to start again, then stops. She puts her hand over her mouth and looks ill.*)

MOUSE: I think she's going to be sick, Molly ...

MOLLY: Anna ...

(ANNA *recovers and recites grandly, bottle in hand.*)

ANNA: 'Paradise is closing down, my friend, and only soldiers
and police and one frightened voter pitched up for the
Final Sale, locking up and cocking guns.
And in the only sunbeam somewhere on the sand lies a
little child with a bullet in his head and a stone in his hand
While back in the Mother City round dinner and TV with
wine and food and fashion we frightened angels of death
beat our wings in time to the requiem;
(MOLLY *has heard this all before and sits patiently.*)
But the sun is gone forever
And the birds will cry till they die in the dark
And the empty landscape . . . and the empty
landscape . . .

MOLLY: 'And the empty landscape of shame and anger colours the
soil red and the sky black'! OK, Anna! Wash your face!
(ANNA *stands and sways. Stares at* MOLLY. *Moves her mouth soundlessly.*)

MOUSE: Here it comes, Molly . . .
(ANNA *is going to be sick.* MOLLY *jumps up and turns* ANNA *towards the door.*)

MOLLY: Not in here! bathroom, Anna, BATHROOM!
(ANNA *exits. She is sick off.* MOLLY *sits, furious.*)

MOLLY: I won't have her staying over here tonight in her state. She trots out the chip on her shoulder and stands on her political soapbox and talks utter crap!

MOUSE: It's always over after the poem, Molly.

MOLLY: No, after the poem she starts on me! I don't need that in my life. Go on, take her home with you. The party's over.

MOUSE: I don't have space for her.

MOLLY: Then make space for her! She's not staying here!

MOUSE: Can't she take your car?

MOLLY: Nobody takes my car. I've worked damn hard for my car and my clothes and my security. I don't have an Afrikaner background, or a rich Daddy, or a dead hero's military pension. You can take that sleeping-bag that whatshisname left here. I don't want it.

MOUSE: But Molly, I've no space . . .

MOLLY: Then sleep in the same bed! She's not that hard up to feel pressed to make a pass at you, dear God!
MOUSE: Don't be disgusting!
MOLLY: And put on some clothes! I hate snivelling losers sitting around kitchens in borrowed dressing-gowns! Go on, get dressed! Don't say I don't care about my friends. And pull yourself together, Mouse, you're supposed to be young and attractive. Get out!
MOUSE: But . . .
(*But* MOLLY *pushes her out of the kitchen.*)
MOLLY: Get out! (*Pause.*) Oh, I hate this place, I think I'll move. (*She sits. The silence overpowers her. She picks up the phone and dials.*) Hello? Hello! Is that Freddie? This line is terrible . . . hello, Freddie? It's Molly! What? Damn . . . Molly! Oh, that's better . . . terrible line, typical. Who's that? Jeremy? Do I know you? Molly. You know me? Oh, has he? What did he say about me? Listen, I'm over sixteen . . . twenty-two, I swear to God! What did Freddie say? OK, you don't have to tell me if you don't want to. Where is the bastard? Oh . . . oh yes, he told me – with whatshername? Ivan? My God, has he gone gay? Hey? Gay! Oh, never mind. No! Don't say I phoned!
(*During this* WILLIAM *comes out of his hiding-place and edges across the kitchen behind her, towards the door.*)
Listen, Jeremy . . . Jeremy . . . that's a nice name. Hey? Jeremy! It's a nice name. Ha, ha, flattery usually gets me everywhere. No, nothing. Just sitting around. And you? Want to come around Loader Street? Yes, come round and we'll . . . hey? Did he tell you that? Yes, I've got some here . . . you want to come round for a snortette? Oh. No. Oh. *Ja*, sure. No, no, it's OK. No, fuck off and enjoy yourself, you bastard! (*She slams the phone down. Pause.*) Oh no . . . why do you do that . . . why do you always do that! (*She turns and sees* WILLIAM *at the door.*) How the hell did you get in!
WILLIAM: I was here earlier . . .
MOLLY: Anna!
WILLIAM: No, it's OK, really . . .
MOLLY: Mouse!
WILLIAM: You said come to the front door. You said you weren't

ashamed of receiving coloureds. Isn't that what you said? (*Pause.*)

MOLLY: What do you want here?
WILLIAM: I came earlier. I talked to you, remember?
MOLLY: Yes, yes, but I don't know you.
WILLIAM: But we talked.
MOLLY: What's that got to do with it?
(*Pause.*)
WILLIAM: I left my bag of greens here.
MOLLY: What?
WILLIAM: These carrots and things.
MOLLY: Is that why you came back?
WILLIAM: I'm sorry.
MOLLY: Were you so desperate for carrots and lettuce and onions that you come creeping around here in the middle of the night, scaring me to death? I might have been sleeping!
WILLIAM: I was around . . .
MOLLY: Oh? What were you doing up here? There's nothing here for you.
WILLIAM: I was up the road.
MOLLY: Doing what?
WILLIAM: Old Sarah. I went to see her.
MOLLY: Aren't you a bit young for all that?
WILLIAM: For what?
MOLLY: Paying for it?
WILLIAM: Sarah is an old friend of my family.
MOLLY: Lovely friends your family has.
WILLIAM: My family used to live in this house. We know her from those days.
MOLLY: I see.
WILLIAM: Old Sarah's a good person.
MOLLY: So am I, but I should be so lucky to have half her visitors.
WILLIAM: I'm here.
MOLLY: Yes. So you are. (*Pause.*) Well, so how do you like your old home? A bit better than you remember it?
WILLIAM: Very nice.
MOLLY: Very nice? Don't tell me you had all this? Fridge, deep-

freeze, microwave, home computer, underfloor heating.
WILLIAM: Underfloor heating?
MOLLY: For winter.
WILLIAM: It doesn't get that cold.
MOLLY: It does now. It leaks like hell and there's a crack in the wall.
WILLIAM: Sloppy plasterwork.
MOLLY: Oh, an architect?
WILLIAM: Not yet.
MOLLY: 'Not yet', excuse me. Are you at university?
WILLIAM: High school.
MOLLY: Aren't you a bit old for school?
WILLIAM: It takes longer for some of us.
MOLLY: You look quite bright to me.
WILLIAM: That's the problem.
　　(*Pause.*)
MOLLY: Mmmm. You got rabbits?
WILLIAM: Rabbits?
MOLLY: Bunny rabbits! I mean, what are the carrots for? Listen, I'm a sophisticated woman and I've seen it all, but carrots? What do you do with carrots?
WILLIAM: We eat them.
MOLLY: Oh? And what else is in the bag?
WILLIAM: Why don't you come and have a look, madam?
MOLLY: Don't be cheeky, boy.
　　(*Pause.* MOLLY *is being seductive.* WILLIAM *looks into the bag.*)
WILLIAM: Squash, potatoes, onions, lettuce and . . .
MOLLY: . . . and the dear little carrots.
WILLIAM: They're quite big.
MOLLY: Mmmm. A real bachelor-boy.
WILLIAM: I like it that way.
MOLLY: Old Sarah's girls must've exhausted you.
WILLIAM: No, I didn't . . .
MOLLY: Oh, tough guy. After an all-night romp with Sarah's bargain-basement beauties, now you come window-shopping up here?
WILLIAM: You're really funny.

MOLLY: Want to see my jokes?

(ANNA *enters, sobered up, with* MOUSE *in tow.*)

ANNA: The bathroom is now free if you want to wash it before you eat it, Molly.

MOLLY: Oh, bugger off!

ANNA: The carrots!

MOLLY: This is ... er ... Carlo.

ANNA: Of course.

MOLLY: He brought me some vegetables.

ANNA: For tonight's meal, no doubt?

MOLLY: Yes, for tonight's meal.

MOUSE: Molly, I think ...

WILLIAM: It's OK.

MOLLY: Thank you, Carlo, you're a treasure.

ANNA: Carlo? I'm Anna.

WILLIAM: Anna.

ANNA: And that's Molly.

WILLIAM: Yes, I know.

MOLLY: There, you see! Carlo, pop round some other time, we're just on our way out.

ANNA: Nonsense, we're not going anywhere.

MOLLY: We're going out!

ANNA: Here, Carlo, have some wine.

MOLLY: We'll be late.

ANNA: For what? Carlo? Wine?

(*Pause.* WILLIAM *looks at* MOUSE, *then at the others. Then he decides.*)

WILLIAM: OK.

(ANNA *pours him a glass of wine.* WILLIAM *sits, holding the bag against him.*)

ANNA: Good. Here. Now what about some delicious sweet-and-sour pork to go with Molly's nice fresh carrots!

(*She takes the bag from him. He holds on to it.*)

Come now, boy, this is a civilized place. Coats, hats and bags stay at the door.

MOUSE: I'll hold it ...

(MOUSE *takes the bag from* WILLIAM *slowly. He lets go.*)

MOLLY: Anna, what do you think you're doing!
ANNA: You like cold Chinese takeaway, Carlo?
WILLIAM: It's OK.
ANNA: OK then, eat. This is Molly's kitchen. You can't ever go away hungry. Everyone always has a good meal here, especially our Molly.
MOLLY: Carlo has to go, Anna, please don't interfere!
ANNA: Oh no, where does Carlo have to go? Carlo? You see, Molly, the boy's hungry. The mouth is full. Don't expect a miracle, let it eat. It's so young and hungry. It needs its strength! Oh, I love watching young men eat. It's so sexy!
MOLLY: Christ, Anna!
ANNA: Tin, Molly!

(ANNA *sits next to* WILLIAM *and patronizes him lovingly*.)

Nice food? Gosh, I had a brother you know, Carlo, who used to eat us out of house and home, until he was killed. A loaf a day. You like bread? Shame, Molly's only got cake. My brother never put on weight, because he was healthy and strong, like you. I mean, take Molly. She sees a crust and blows up like a petrol-bomb, but my brother had a hard, flat stomach. Do you have a hard stomach?

(*She slowly feels his stomach*.)

Oh yes, a nice hard body. Molly, come and feel the boy's body. It's so hard.

(WILLIAM *stares at her*.)

Don't let me interrupt you, Carlo. Finish your last spoonful. Think of all the poor starving children. Mustn't waste... (*Then she empties the leftovers on Molly's plate on to* WILLIAM's.) There we are. Waste not, want more.
MOLLY: That's my plate!
ANNA: He won't catch it from the plate. And where are you from, Carlo? Your name sounds Italian, but you look like a common old coloured boy to me. Don't answer with your mouth full. You'll choke and die and Molly will kill herself! Yes, 'Carlo' sounds Italian. I like Italians. I also like coloureds. In theory, of course. Don't really count any among my friends, but Molly always says how lovely they are. She should know, treating her

coloured maid like a piece of shit. Sit down, Molly, you'll wear down your heels. Now don't rush, there's lots of time.

MOLLY: What the hell do you think you're doing?

ANNA: I'm being nice. I can, you know, it's part of my Christian national education. I can look the angel of death in the face and be nice.

(*She takes the spoon from* WILLIAM, *and while she sings a children's lullaby, she feeds him. On the third mouthful he refuses to take it. Pause.*)

The boy is finished. Take away his plate, Molly, and wash it nicely. We don't want to overburden poor Mrs Peters on Monday. Now, Carlo, how about a cigarette?

WILLIAM: Thanks.

ANNA: Give him a cigarette, Molly.

MOUSE: Anna, I think we'd better . . .

ANNA: You give him a cigarette, Mouse!

(MOUSE *offers* WILLIAM *a box of filter cigarettes. He slowly takes one.*)

WILLIAM: Do you have plain?

ANNA: Do we have plain? Of course we have plain!

(*She takes the cigarette, breaks off the filter and presents the 'plain' cigarette back to him.*)

Give him a light, Molly.

WILLIAM: It's OK, I've got a light.

(*He takes out a cheap plastic lighter.*)

ANNA: Nice lighter.

WILLIAM: Oh?

ANNA: Beautiful. Just like the one you had, Mouse.

MOUSE: What?

ANNA: The lighter. Let me see? What a coincidence, Mouse, just like the lighter I gave you.

MOUSE: No, mine was a Dunhill . . .

ANNA: Don't be grand, Mouse. Your lighter was just like this one. It was even the same colour, just like this one. You know, Carlo, Mouse had a lighter just like this one.

WILLIAM: Really?

ANNA: Till tonight, that is. She ... 'lost' it. Where did you get this lighter, Carlo?
WILLIAM: I bought it.
ANNA: Really? You bought it.
MOUSE: Anna, it's nothing like mine!
ANNA: But I gave you yours. I should know.
MOUSE: What the hell are you doing?
ANNA: I'm being nice. (*Pause*.) So, Carlo, tell me, do you drive?
MOUSE: Anna.
WILLIAM: I don't have a licence.
ANNA: But you do drive?
WILLIAM: I can.
MOUSE: Molly, stop this!
MOLLY: Anna, this is getting boring!
ANNA: Shut up, Molly. Can you drive an automatic?
WILLIAM: My uncle has an automatic Chev.
ANNA: Really?
WILLIAM: I used to drive that when I was a kid.
ANNA: Good price for cars like that.
MOLLY: Stop it, you sordid bitch! Leave the boy alone!
ANNA: But I'm just saying to his face what you've been saying behind his back. 'It's the coloureds'! OK, there's 'the coloureds'!
MOUSE: How can you accuse him of these things?
ANNA: But he's been accused and convicted. You said he's guilty!
MOLLY: Carlo, you'd better go ...
MOUSE: You can prove nothing!
ANNA: Here's the proof! What's a coloured doing up here in a white area?
MOUSE: Why must you simplify everything?
ANNA: Simplify everything?
MOUSE: This was his home!
ANNA: Exactly. And what is happening out there? Affectionate homage to white rule? You were terrified!
MOUSE: Yes, but at last something is happening! Whatever it is, at least thank God it's started to happen!
(WILLIAM *laughs*.)

ANNA: Are you laughing at us?
WILLIAM: To think some of us are scared of you! You're just funny.
ANNA: Funny?
WILLIAM: *Ja.*
ANNA: You think you can just laugh and it will all fall in your lap?
WILLIAM: I don't live around here any more.
ANNA: Then you'd better start working for the privilege, boy! Hey, boy!

(*She nudges him, trying to provoke him.*)

You want to live here again? Boy? So do something! Steal something! Kill someone! I dare you! Make us hate! Help us to hate!

MOUSE: Anna, stop it!
ANNA: Here. Take! Help yourself . . . go on . . . take . . . take!!!

(MOUSE *is in the way.* ANNA *viciously pushes* MOUSE *at* WILLIAM. *He catches her and holds her.* ANNA *pulls out drawers from the sideboard and throws the contents on the floor – towels, cutlery, place-mats – saying as she does it*)

Take . . . take . . . take . . . take!

(*Then she slowly sinks to the floor and hunches, sobbing.* MOLLY *stands horrified, staring at* ANNA. *Pause.*)

WILLIAM: Pass me a glass of water, please . . .
MOUSE: It's OK. I'm OK. Are you OK?
WILLIAM: *Ja.*
MOLLY: Anna?

(MOUSE *goes to* ANNA *and helps her up gently.*)

ANNA: Mousie, I'm sorry . . . I'm sorry . . .

(ANNA *looks at* MOLLY *and* WILLIAM, *then exits. After a moment* MOLLY *follows her.*)

MOLLY: Anna?

(MOLLY *exits.*)

WILLIAM: What was all that about?

(MOUSE *starts clearing up the mess, repacking drawers.*)

MOUSE: I'm sorry about all this. Anna's very tense. Her brother was killed in the township.
WILLIAM: Oh.

MOUSE: And Molly still loves her ex-husband, but he's got another, younger wife.
WILLIAM: Oh.
MOUSE: And Anna's car was stolen.
WILLIAM: I see, so she thought it was me?
MOUSE: Well, you see, my room was burgled.
WILLIAM: It sounds like you've had a hell of a party!
(MOUSE *shrugs and smiles.*)
MOUSE: Saturday night.
MOLLY: (*Off*) Mouse?
WILLIAM: Is your friend all right?
MOUSE: Remorse. Very Afrikaans.
WILLIAM: You could've told them, you know.
(MOUSE *looks into the bag and takes out the gun carefully.*)
MOUSE: I was going to. But then when they were so horrible to you . . .
WILLIAM: I'm a big boy, you know.
MOUSE: . . . I wanted to use this. How can you be so calm?
WILLIAM: I can handle women.
MOUSE: Oh.
MOLLY: (*Off*) Mouse, you'd better drive her home in my car.
MOUSE: I'll have to go.
(*She puts the gun in the bag and hands the bag to him.*)
WILLIAM: Can you drive all right?
MOUSE: I used to drive Land Rovers in Rhodesia. Do you want a lift?
WILLIAM: No thanks.
MOUSE: Your buses have stopped. I believe there's a lot of shooting in your areas.
WILLIAM: Yes.
MOUSE: Are you very involved in all this?
WILLIAM: Yes.
MOUSE: Would you use that?
WILLIAM: I hope not. You see, my sister was shot by the police this morning. That's why I came to see my ma. That's why she left early. I've actually come to ask Molly to advance us some money on Ma's wages.
MOUSE: Oh my God, William . . .

(*She is overcome. Looks at him.* MOLLY *enters quickly.*)

MOLLY: Mouse, come on, and stop that eternal snivelling! Anna's waiting in the car!

(*She pushes* MOUSE *out of the room and calls after her.*)

And for the tin's sake, drive carefully, we've had enough excitement for tonight. Phone me tomorrow after eleven. And Mouse? Don't take the freeway! Those damn kids are throwing stones at the cars! (*She sighs and sits.*) Jesus van der Christ!

WILLIAM: Tin.

MOLLY: Hey?

WILLIAM: You said a swear-word. Tin.

MOLLY: No, that wasn't a swear-word. And, anyway, what do you mean, 'tin'? I don't even know you!

WILLIAM: Aren't I Carlo?

MOLLY: Are you?

(*Pause. A siren passes outside.*)

Ow . . . I've got that pain here over my heart again . . .

WILLIAM: Go and see a doctor.

MOLLY: I need to pay a specialist good money to hear that all I need is love and affection? I can get that from a vet.

(WILLIAM *picks up some of the cutlery lying on the floor.*)

Leave that. The maid will be in tomorrow.

WILLIAM: Sunday?

MOLLY: Whenever.

(*He collects the plates from the table.*)

Old habits die hard, hey? Careful of those plates. They're from Poland. Belonged to my grandmother. She was an incredible person.

WILLIAM: So was mine.

MOLLY: Well, at least we've got something in common. (*She looks at him keenly.*) So, aren't you just dying to see the rest of the house?

WILLIAM: It's very late.

MOLLY: Yes. Well then, let's start with my bedroom. (*She holds out her hand to him.*) Come on, 'Carlo'. And leave the carrots. They'll still be here tomorrow morning.

(*He goes to her. She expects a kiss. He stops and looks at her.*)

Be nice to me...
(*He walks out of the door. The front door slams.* MOLLY *stands alone. Blackout.*)

THE END

Panorama

Panorama was first performed at the Grahamstown Festival on 5 July 1987, directed by Pieter-Dirk Uys with Lynne Maree (ROSA), Susan Coetzer-Opperman (KARIN), Richard van der Westhuizen (GROBBELAAR) and Thoko Ntshinga (SIBI).

Characters

———————— o ————————

ROSA
KARIN
GROBBELAAR
SIBI MAKHALE

The play is set on Robben Island in Table Bay, from where there is a view on to Table Mountain and the city of Cape Town.

The action takes place in a small, carefully decorated sitting-room. There is a couch looking out at the audience – i.e. the window – and a table and three chairs directly behind it. There is a large blocked picture of Table Mountain, seen from across the bay, on the wall, some colourful children's drawings of the panorama and a fish tank containing two goldfish.

The time is now.

Act One

———————— o ————————

KARIN *is on the couch, fiddling with a portable tape recorder.*

KARIN: Hello? Testing one, two, one, two ... oh, hell's bells, what have I done wrong ... hello? Ah. (*It records.*) Hello, Mummy, it's me again, Karin. How are you? I hope you remembered Aunt Esme's birthday last week – she is older than you, isn't she? I sent her a few postcards of the panorama, I hope she likes them. It's so long since I've been over to Cape Town, because the sea is so rough ... anyway, I couldn't go and look for any new postcards for your collection, but I asked Rosa to have a look. She goes over quite often. (*Pauses the machine*) What else ... (*Takes a bite of a sandwich*) Mummy ... (*Switches on machine*) It's a perfect day. No wind. The panorama here from our sitting-room is too wonderful – look at your postcards and imagine you're here. It's just like your postcards. Actually, not quite. Most of those pictures were taken from places on the mainland, but they say the view from here is the best, because we're far away enough to get the whole of Table Mountain in and everything. Looks quite unnatural. Funny when you think that the old explorers, like Jan van Riebeeck, sailed into Table Bay and saw all this beauty for the first time – of course, without those three horrible tower blocks up against the mountain, or the cableway ... and, of course, the prison wasn't here. (*Stops and rewinds: listens to herself*) '... of course, without those three horrible tower blocks up against the mountain, or the cableway ... and, of course, the prison wasn't here'. (*Records again*) Oh no, Mummy, I just listened to myself and I sound so awful ...

GROBBELAAR: (*Off*) Miss Rosa?

KARIN: Oh no, there's that baboon of a Grobbelaar again. Always sniffing around after Rosa. (*Switches off machine*) She's not here!

(GROBBELAAR *enters.*)

GROBBELAAR: Oh, hello, Miss Karin. Where's Miss Rosa?

KARIN: She had to take detention at school today. Want a sandwich?

GROBBELAAR: I had lunch with the other warders.

KARIN: Shame, then you must really be hungry. Here.

(*Hands him a piece of her sandwich. He takes it.*)

GROBBELAAR: Thanks. Detention? Today?

KARIN: We two take turns; I took Monday, today's hers. You know that, Grobbelaar.

GROBBELAAR: Oh yes.

KARIN: I don't think there will be many kids: it's rugby practice. Our little boys are playing against Milnerton on Saturday.

GROBBELAAR: Our under-twelve team is much better than that lot across the bay.

KARIN: *Ja*. Well, rugby is king, so I don't suppose Rosa will be very late.

GROBBELAAR: *Ja*, rugby's the best.

KARIN: *Ja*. Who cut your hair?

GROBBELAAR: It's my day off.

KARIN: Why don't you go over to Cape Town? It's a lovely day . . .

GROBBELAAR: Hey, the new window really makes a difference.

KARIN: Yes, now we can see the Milnerton and the Mouille Point lighthouses without even moving our positions on the couch.

GROBBELAAR: Hey? No, I was over in Cape Town last weekend. I don't have a nice time there any more.

KARIN: But don't you have friends there?

GROBBELAAR: *Ja*, but they're always on patrol in the black townships nowadays. Anyway, it's not so nice even with them.

KARIN: Not so nice as what, Grobbelaar? A nice girl?

GROBBELAAR: Miss Karin?

KARIN: Grobbelaar, man, you should really get yourself a nice girlfriend. You know Rosa won't go out with you.

GROBBELAAR: She teaches.

KARIN: Oh no, even if she was free. She told you: she's got a boyfriend up in Johannesburg. I know she has. They write to each other often.
GROBBELAAR: Really.
KARIN: Yes. So, Grobbelaar, why don't you look around for someone else?
GROBBELAAR: Who?
KARIN: Who? Isn't there someone here that you ... er ... you know?
GROBBELAAR: I was hoping Miss Rosa would come with me next month. They've got another nice function at work. Dinner and a dance. The hall will be all decorated with streamers and things, like last year, remember?
KARIN: *Ja.*
GROBBELAAR: There will also be a band.
KARIN: Sounds nice.
GROBBELAAR: I thought Miss Rosa would like it.
KARIN: You know Rosa won't go with you.
GROBBELAAR: But I can still ask. What's on the bread?
KARIN: Peanut butter.
GROBBELAAR: Hey? I used to eat it a lot when I was small. Black Cat Peanut Butter. I like it.
KARIN: Thank you. Want some more?
GROBBELAAR: If it's not too much trouble.

(KARIN *exits pleased.* GROBBELAAR *snoops around: studies the full bottle of whisky. He creeps up to the goldfish and gives them a fright. Then he rewinds the tape and listens.*)

TAPE: '... oh no, Mummy, I just listened to myself and I sound so awful ...'
'Miss Rosa?'
'Oh no, there's that baboon of a Grobbelaar again. Always sniffing around after Rosa.'
GROBBELAAR: Baboon, hey? (*He laughs.*)
(KARIN *enters with a plate and sandwich.*)
KARIN: So, Grobbelaar, what are you going to do today?
GROBBELAAR: I don't know; maybe they need me at work. Today they brought in a new lot. Two white girls.

KARIN: Here. Brown bread. It's better for you.

GROBBELAAR: Funny, when I started working here it was just Kaffirs.

KARIN: I wonder, yes...

GROBBELAAR: *Ja.*

(*Pause.* KARIN *looks out at the view.*)

KARIN: Looks so peaceful.

GROBBELAAR: We heard about some more shooting out in the black townships. Two bombs.

KARIN: Really? You people hear all about these things?

GROBBELAAR: Yes. So how's it at school?

KARIN: Oh, can't complain.

GROBBELAAR: Lots of work?

KARIN: The usual. And you?

GROBBELAAR: Also. Sometimes I really wish someone would try to escape, just to make the day a little more exciting.

KARIN: How could they escape?

GROBBELAAR: Impossible. But I just thought, wondered...

KARIN: No, but how could people escape from here?

GROBBELAAR: Impossible.

KARIN: Swim?

GROBBELAAR: Too cold. No, they didn't choose this place for no reason.

KARIN: Not for the panorama.

GROBBELAAR: No. Nice sandwich.

KARIN: You'll get fat... I'm just joking...

GROBBELAAR: Hey?

KARIN: OK, Grobbelaar, I'll tell Rosa you came round visiting.

GROBBELAAR: *Ja*, no, it's OK.

(*But he doesn't go. Pause.*)

GROBBELAAR: Will they get married? Miss Rosa and that man from Johannesburg?

KARIN: Maybe.

GROBBELAAR: I'd like to get married. Kids. Nice house. But not here. This place is no good for kids. Too much wind.

KARIN: *Ja.* I'm going to give this place another year at the most and then I want to find a position somewhere else.

GROBBELAAR: Hey? I'll miss you, Miss Karin.
KARIN: Really.
(ROSA *is heard off in a fury*.)
ROSA: Shit! One day I swear I'll answer him back in spite of his rank and uniform. (*She enters*.) Why am I such a coward? I'm not even in the force. Karin, you could've asked me. It always happens: I make all the speeches in my head and say 'Go to hell' and resign, and then when I'm there in real life and let rip, I go all cute-cute and say 'Love to your wife'. Why am I always bowing and scraping? 'Yes, sir' this, 'No, sir' that! The job's shit; the pay? That's a laugh. Hello, Grobbelaar, do you live here now?
GROBBELAAR: Hello, Miss Rosa. Sorry, Miss?
ROSA: And what are you eating?
KARIN: Peanut-butter sandwich. I made him one.
(*She looks at the view*.)
ROSA: And look at that old cow grinning at me from Devils Peak to Lion's Head! (*Turns on* KARIN) You could've at least asked me, Karin. I mean, we *do* live together in this house and it's not exactly a mansion. I don't mind for one night. Shit, the whole thing around here is heavy enough as it is with the prison and the security and the secrets and now on top of it weeping relatives – but, please, you could've asked me. I would've probably said yes – eventually.
KARIN: Oh?
ROSA: Don't look so surprised. Generosity isn't one of my strong points, but I've also got the wobblies that pass for feelings. Hey, Grobbelaar, damn it, man, you've dropped crumbs all over the floor!
GROBBELAAR: Sorry, Miss...
ROSA: Don't they feed you down there? Must you come here and eat us out of house and home? We're only teachers! No jackpot, you know...
GROBBELAAR: Hell, Miss Rosa, I'm really sorry...
KARIN: Never mind, Grobbelaar, she's just joking.
(*She helps him with the crumbs*.)
ROSA: Ow... God, I felt my back go when I was demonstrating

self-defence to the nine-year-old girls. Protection against molestation, Grobbelaar.

(*He gives an embarrassed laugh. She fixes him with a stare.*)

ROSA: You've had your . . . what is it? Shaved off your moustache?

GROBBELAAR: I never had a moustache.

ROSA: Beard?

KARIN: He's cut his hair.

ROSA: Going over to town? Have you also got part-time work in the townships?

GROBBELAAR: No, I'm full-time here. Miss Rosa, I was wondering if . . .

ROSA: Karin, I think I'll go over on Saturday morning and spend the weekend . . .

KARIN: Me too?

ROSA: And vomit all the way back and forth? Anyway, my boyfriend is coming down from Jo'burg.

KARIN: Oh.

ROSA: Then I can get the last boat on Sunday.

GROBBELAAR: I might also be on that boat, Miss Rosa.

ROSA: Amazing. Don't get up, Grobbelaar, feel at home.

(*But* GROBBELAAR *does get up.*)

GROBBELAAR: I also get up at home. It's good manners.

ROSA: There's something wrong with the sink. Would you have a look at it before you go?

GROBBELAAR: Of course, Miss Rosa.

KARIN: You don't mind, do you, Grobbelaar?

GROBBELAAR: No, Miss Rosa. Any time.

(*He exits.*)

ROSA: I bet he pulls the wings off baby flies and laughs!

KARIN: Oh shame, Rosa, he's quite sweet, really.

ROSA: OK. So where do we put her?

KARIN: Who?

ROSA: Where does she sleep? I'm not giving up my bed for anyone, that's for sure.

KARIN: Who?

ROSA: I thought you'd know her name. You're the one who said yes.

KARIN: No.

ROSA: No? They said you said it was OK. Karin, the girl coming to stay over tonight! The copshop said you agreed.

KARIN: Where did they get that? I said nothing!

ROSA: So I said, well, OK, if you say it's OK, it's OK.

KARIN: I didn't say it was OK! What are you talking about?

ROSA: She's coming to see someone who's inside.

KARIN: And she's staying here with us?

ROSA: We said yes, didn't we?

KARIN: Oh no, I don't like having these people's relatives here, Rosa. They make me nervous.

ROSA: Oh, come on, this place isn't a leper colony any more. They're just people like me and you. Not quite like him in there, but then there was also only one King Kong.

KARIN: Can't she go and stay somewhere else? With the doctor or the principal or whoever? They've got the space.

ROSA: I suppose so. You tell them.

KARIN: Me?

ROSA: You tell them that you don't want her here and can't she stay with Doctor Hugo or Mr Pierce.

KARIN: Never. (*Pause*.) I suppose she could sleep in here, couldn't she? You did say it was only for one night, hey?

ROSA: And what about me? Where do I sit tonight? You know I like to watch the panorama before I go to bed. Where do I sit? The kitchen? Like hell, just because you've handed over my comforts to a stranger.

(KARIN *thinks for a moment*.)

KARIN: Grobbelaar said some white student-types were brought in this morning, two girls. *Ja*, well, in that case I suppose she can have my room, I don't mind. I'll sleep in here once you've looked at the panorama and all that. I'll read.

ROSA: Well, that's your own business. I just don't want to be mucked about, OK?

KARIN: OK.

(GROBBELAAR *enters beaming*.)

GROBBELAAR: All fixed like new, Miss Rosa.

ROSA: What?

GROBBELAAR: The sink. Tea-leaves. Use tea-bags.

KARIN: Thanks, Grobbelaar.
ROSA: One of my small luxuries in life is a pot of real tea.
KARIN: We usually throw the tea-leaves outside in the garden.
GROBBELAAR: That's good.
ROSA: Well, I'm going to take that bath now.
   (*She exits.*)
GROBBELAAR: Is she cross with me?
KARIN: No, man, Grobbelaar. It's just your bosses cheated us into taking someone in for the night. She's cross about that. I'm also cross.
GROBBELAAR: *Ja*, but you know we don't have facilities here for people who want to spend the night. Except in the cells.
   (*He laughs.*)
KARIN: Well, you people should create decent facilities.
GROBBELAAR: Listen, maybe someone's going to die. When they can't move them over to the mainland they let the family come over and say goodbye. Or maybe it's got something to do with those white detainees. You know they've got money, those Jews – fancy lawyers.
KARIN: Please, I really don't want to know, Grobbelaar. I refuse to listen. Just look out at that mountain and forget all the ugly things in the world, because that there is out of God's hands and that's the reality, Grobbelaar – that mass of rock and granite and the sea and the sky and the sun. That's what it's all about.
GROBBELAAR: Yes, Miss Karin. Maybe that's why we're here, hey? To make sure that what's over there stays there.
KARIN: What?
GROBBELAAR: No, I'm thinking suddenly. That's what happens to me when I get mixed up with you teacher-types.
KARIN: Oh.
GROBBELAAR: Yes.
   (*Pause. They look out at the view.*)
GROBBELAAR: Miss Karin, can I ask you a big favour?
KARIN: Yes.
GROBBELAAR: This function at work, you know? The dance?
KARIN: Yes. Thank you!
GROBBELAAR: Tell Miss Rosa she'll really have a nice time.

KARIN: Oh. OK.
(GROBBELAAR *exits*.)
KARIN: Anyway, I don't even like dancing ...
(ROSA *enters*.)
ROSA: Is he gone?
KARIN: Yes.
ROSA: I wish he'd find a nice mousey-looking Afrikaans girl with thick ankles and marry her and move to South America. What's this function he's talking about?
KARIN: At the prison. A dance with a band.
ROSA: Grim.
KARIN: Is a public holiday coming up, or what?
ROSA: Forget it.
KARIN: Shame. He did fix the sink, Rosa.
ROSA: So let's restrict his plumbing to the sink.
KARIN: What?
ROSA: Never mind. Your usual?
KARIN: Hell's bells, no, I shouldn't ...
(*But she does.* ROSA *pours them each a drink*.)
ROSA: So how was your day?
KARIN: Oh, same as always. My Boer War maps still haven't come from Pretoria, you know.
ROSA: Maybe they still need them.
KARIN: Oh. And you?
ROSA: They still haven't fixed that damn window in my room. Thank God there was no wind today. Mmmm, looks quite clear for a change.
KARIN: It's so beautiful ...
ROSA: Any post?
KARIN: No, but I'm sure I'll get a letter soon. They don't take that long to decide.
ROSA: Don't you know the Department yet? Karin, I think you would've heard from them if you'd got that job.
KARIN: *Ja*. Maybe I still will.
ROSA: I hope so for your sake. Cheers.
KARIN: It's not so bad here: fresh air, nice house. Nice people.
ROSA: Well, I suppose I could've been stuck somewhere north of

Pretoria with a general class IQ of ten. I should be grateful. What's for supper?

KARIN: I got a nice fish...

ROSA: Not fish again!

KARIN: Fish cakes!

ROSA: Did you buy some new tomato sauce? OK. I suppose we'll have to feed her.

KARIN: There'll be enough food for three. Grobbelaar says they only allow family to come when someone's dying. Maybe that's why she's coming. It really makes me nervous.

ROSA: Look, she sleeps here and then she goes and we don't have to be involved. We just remind the powers-that-be of our sacrifice, send them a bill for bed and breakfast and fish cakes and ask to have the front of the cottage repainted and a strong trellis put up for my red bougainvillaea – which I know won't grow in the wind, but we can still try.

KARIN: *Ja*, and just when it flowers, I'll get that new job and have to leave and miss out on all the nice times and everything.

ROSA: And no white paint! I'm sick of all this over-emphasis. This time I want something really modern.

KARIN: Chocolate-brown or dark green... where's that magazine...?

ROSA: Something with class. I might lose my mind out here, but I'll be damned if I'm also going to lose my taste! (*Sees the tape recorder*) Talking to your ma?

KARIN: Just started. I feel so terrible, I've done nothing for weeks.

ROSA: Give her my love.

(*A knock on the door.*)

ROSA: What's this now...

(GROBBELAAR *enters.*)

ROSA: You're too early, we're not eating yet.

GROBBELAAR: Miss Rosa?

ROSA: And please stop calling me Miss Rosa! I get that all day from the kids in class: 'miss' this and 'miss' that!

GROBBELAAR: OK, miss. Listen, I shouldn't be doing this, you know, it's my day off. But the sergeant knows I'm a good friend of yours, so he said for me to come down here and bring the girl and tell you the rules.

KARIN: She's here?

GROBBELAAR: No, wait, Miss Karin. She's outside. But first the rules.

ROSA: What rules?

GROBBELAAR: There are rules, Miss Rosa. You see, when she comes into the room when I'm still here, then you both must leave. If I'm not here, then only one of you has to leave. And when you two want to be in the room together, like now — then she must leave.

(*Pause. The women take this in.*)

KARIN: Is that supposed to be a joke?

ROSA: What the hell are you talking about, Grobbelaar? We make the arrangements here, if you don't mind. She'll sleep in Karin's room, so there's no need for anyone to leave. You bloody police — who the hell do you think you are, anyway?

GROBBELAAR: She can only be allowed in a room with one other person at the same time. No, man, Miss Karin, tell her it's the rules.

KARIN: But I don't understand, Grobbelaar, is she sick?

GROBBELAAR: No, Miss Karin, she's just a banned person.

ROSA: I don't believe it!

KARIN: What? Why?

GROBBELAAR: Hey?

KARIN: Why is she banned? What did she do?

GROBBELAAR: Nothing, she's just banned.

ROSA: Well, I'm not moving, banned person or not. So you can take her straight back to the copshop and let them put her up for the night. I want nothing to do with this!

KARIN: You mean only one person in the same room everywhere? Even in her own house? With her own family? But that must be a joke!

ROSA: This is not her house. This is my house.

KARIN: Yes, this is our house.

GROBBELAAR: She's just a banned person. I don't know why. We don't have to know these things, just that she's banned. But they usually have a good reason. It's not for us to question.

ROSA: I question!

KARIN: But why isn't she locked up like the others? Why do they let her wander around free?

GROBBELAAR: They usually restrict them to certain areas and so make them harmless. This is a special case, Miss, the sergeant said so.

KARIN: No, but listen, isn't there a pamphlet or something to explain it all properly to us? I don't want to break any laws. Hey, Rosa?

ROSA: I just don't believe it!

GROBBELAAR: It will be all right, Miss Karin. Miss Rosa, it's only for twenty-four hours. She's got a permit to leave her restricted area, but she must be back there in twenty-four hours. Listen, if you want to come down to the sergeant, he'll explain it all to you, but it's really very easy. Just one person at a time and – oh yes, she may not address any meetings.

ROSA: Bang goes tonight's PTA! Wait for me, Grobbelaar, I'm coming with you!

GROBBELAAR: To the function?

ROSA: To the office! And bugger the sergeant – I want to talk to someone who's really in charge. There is a limit!
(*She exits.*)

GROBBELAAR: I thought she'd say she'd come with me to the function . . .

KARIN: But what did this girl do?

GROBBELAAR: Probably politics again, Miss Karin. I don' know.

KARIN: Where is she . . .

GROBBELAAR: No, hang on, she's just outside . . . it's OK. She's young. Looks quite clean. Just for this one night, Miss Karin. I know they'll really be grateful at the office, really. I mean, just in case you're applying for a nice new job at another school? I'm sure the sergeant will put in a good word . . .

KARIN: How do you know about that application? No one knows . . .

GROBBELAAR: We'll all put in a good word, Miss Karin, I promise.

KARIN: Did Rosa tell you about that? How do you people know these things?

GROBBELAAR: Shall I bring her in now or what?

KARIN: No, wait . . . Rosa?

(SIBI *enters and stands, impassive. She is wearing dark glasses.*)

GROBBELAAR: Oh yes, I meant to say, she's . . .

KARIN: Oh. (*Pause.*) Grobbelaar?

GROBBELAAR: Sorry, I should've told you sooner.

KARIN: Grobbelaar, we're one too many.

GROBBELAAR: Hey?

KARIN: One, two, three . . .

GROBBELAAR: Oh. Never mind, I'll go. I can stand outside and talk to you through the window, that's OK.

KARIN: No, no, let me rather go . . .

ROSA: (*Off*). . . there are a few pertinent things I have to say to . . .
(*She enters and sees* SIBI. *Stops. Pause.*)

KARIN: And now we're four.

GROBBELAAR: I'll walk you up to the office, Miss Rosa.

ROSA: Is this . . . er . . .

GROBBELAAR: Only for twenty-four hours.

KARIN: There are four of us. Two of us must go. Please! We'll get into trouble!

ROSA: I can't leave the house now . . .

GROBBELAAR: Come, Miss Rosa . . .

ROSA: Will Karin be OK? Maybe she should come too.

KARIN: Yes, I think so . . .

GROBBELAAR: No, Miss Karin, you'll be quite all right. Listen, man, this is Robben Island, the safest place in the world!

(GROBBELAAR *and* ROSA *exit;* ROSA *backs out, visibly concerned. Pause.*)

KARIN: *Ja.* (*Pause.*) Was the sea rough? (*No reaction*) Oh, you're lucky. I get terribly seasick, you know. Can you believe it? Living on an island and always getting terribly seasick? Chronic. *Ja.* That's why I try and avoid going over to Cape Town. I can't face those hours of hell. You're lucky.

(*Pause.* SIBI *just stands and looks at* KARIN. KARIN *desperately looks around for something to talk about.*)

KARIN: *Ja*, it's beautiful when the sea's calm, the mountain is so big and blue, *nê?* And everything's so pretty. That's to say, if there's no wind. A really beautiful view of the mountain from here. Did you see? Rosa calls it our panorama, free from the gods ... (*Pause.*) *Ja*. I used to collect postcards of Table Mountain because each one was so different and colourful. You'll be amazed how many – each one somehow not the same as the others. *Ja*. I sent them all to my mother in the Free State. Shame. She made a big ... what do you call it ... collage! You know, a collage, and hung it in the lounge. I think she must have most of the postcards ever taken by now. I'm sending her a little tape ... So you weren't seasick? That's nice. (*Pause.*) *Ja*. Is this your first visit here? I mean to the Cape? The Cape of Good Hope! (*Pause.*) Why are you a banned person?

SIBI: I'm black.

KARIN: Oh. (*Pause.*) Er ... did you know that this island was a leper colony and all sorts of things like that in the past? They used stone from the quarry here to build the castle in Cape Town. You know, the castle? With its five points: er ... Buren ... Leiden ... Oranje, Katzenellenbogen and ... oh, hell, I teach the children history but I'll never remember all five.

SIBI: Nassau.

KARIN: Of course, Nassau. That's fantastic. Did you finish school and all that?

SIBI: Yes.

KARIN: Fantastic. I really didn't want this job when I applied for it, I mean, I secretly hoped I wouldn't get it, but I did get it and so here I am. It's the water, I suppose. I don't really like the water all that much. (*Looks out of the window*) They say you're only staying till tomorrow. You won't really have a chance to see much of the island. They once built a church here, but there wasn't a preacher. There's a wreck too. Quite a few wrecks.

SIBI: I've come to see my father.

KARIN: Oh, yes.

SIBI: He's sick, they say.
KARIN: Oh, I'm sorry. (*Pause.*) Would you like some tea?
SIBI: No, thanks.
KARIN: Gosh, but she's taking long. (*Pause.*) I'm sure they can put you up in a better place than this ... I mean, hell's bells, it's silly to squeeze you in here. There are much better places. You know, they still don't cater for visitors here. Silly, hey? When will they learn. Is that all you brought?
SIBI: I wasn't allowed more.
KARIN: Oh well, it's only for a day, isn't it? You don't need much for just twenty-four hours – I mean, hell's bells, it's like going over to Cape Town for a weekend. (*Pause.* KARIN *listens desperately for* ROSA's *return.*) I ... er ... I've never met a banned person before.
SIBI: It's no big deal.
KARIN: They all make it sound like ... well, like it's a disease, you know. But one with many rules and do's and dont's ... I mean, you're not a murderer or something, are you? Are you? I just don't know what all the fuss is about ... (*Pause.*) No, hell's bells, I just don't know ...
SIBI: Can I sit down?
KARIN: Of course ... maybe you'd like a cool drink or something? You must be thirsty.
SIBI: Do you have a phone?
KARIN: No, why?
SIBI: Just asking. Do you think I could use your bathroom?
KARIN: For what?
SIBI: I want to go to the toilet.
KARIN: Oh, you want the toilet. Next to the bathroom. But, you know, they'll be back just now, and then you'll be able to have a bath and do everything in proper comfort.
SIBI: I'd rather just wee first, OK? Down the passage to the end?
KARIN: How do you know?
SIBI: I can see it from here.
  (SIBI *exits.* KARIN *sits numbly.*)
KARIN: Oh, hell's bells ... (*Looks out for* ROSA. *She is very disturbed. Looks off to the bathroom. Then she tidies up the room*

and is seen to hide some valuables, i.e. the tape recorder and some ornaments. She checks the money in her bag.) Please, Rosa . . . please hurry . . .
(*She looks off to the left and right down the passage on both sides, wondering who will appear first; then she sees* ROSA *enter.*)

KARIN: Oh, thank God . . . what's happened? Did you tell them? She's in the toilet – I couldn't stop her, she had to go. Did you tell them she can't stay here?

ROSA: Oh yes, I told them she can't stay here, but she's staying all the same.

KARIN: Oh no, we just don't have room for her!

ROSA: Then we'll just have to make room for her. I was ordered – ordered! – to make her stay here as pleasant as possible.

KARIN: For a banned black person, the office ordered you to do that? That's ridiculous!

ROSA: You'd better believe it. They're obviously scared the overseas Press will get hold of another stick to beat us with.

KARIN: Oh no, is the overseas Press also here?

ROSA: We're the local branch of the Holiday Inn.

KARIN: And if we refuse?

ROSA: You refuse. Go on, you tell them no!

KARIN: Never!

ROSA: Here she comes; I want to talk to her.

KARIN: But . . .
(SIBI *enters.*)

ROSA: Make us some tea, Karin.

KARIN: She doesn't want tea . . .

ROSA: *I* want tea.

SIBI: And anyway, three's an illegal gathering.

KARIN: Oh.
(*She exits.*)

ROSA: I'm Rosa.

SIBI: Sibi Makhale.

ROSA: Sibi.

SIBI: My mother was working as a nurse for a Doctor Baker in Soweto when I was born. I was called 'little Cathy Baker'.

C.B. Now we say it quickly with an ethnic twang and it sounds OK. Sibi!

ROSA: I'll be quite honest with you, OK? I've never been interested in politics. I don't mind black people, I never did. I can't say they're my best friends, because, well, I just don't know any. But whatever, I just don't want you here. It's not political or racial or anything. It's just selfish: this place isn't big enough for three. I work hard for my living and I need to relax. And besides all that, I really don't feel like getting involved with your problem, your black power or whatever it is you people stand for.

SIBI: The future?

ROSA: Or smart-arse comments like that. I do my job here and I like my life as it is, and that's that. So. Now you know where you stand.

SIBI: Thank you.

ROSA: I'll of course, within the framework of what's expected of me, try and make your stay here as comfortable as I can. But you're no friend of mine, OK?

SIBI: Sure. Don't worry about me, Miss Rosa. I'll just wait quietly till they come to get me and then I'll quietly go and see my father and quietly go back into obscurity tomorrow and you'll never know I was here. I won't even take the silver.

ROSA: I didn't mean it like that. And don't call me Miss Rosa. You're not one of my pupils. (*Pause.*) What time did they say?

SIBI: They didn't say. (*Pause. She looks out at the view.*) I believe the wind can blow very hard here.

ROSA: A beautiful sight, the cloud over the mountain. The tablecloth.

SIBI: A cruel wind that makes men mad.

ROSA: It just cleans the air.

SIBI: Your air. 'It blows the fine sand through the barbed windows, makes the stone floors rough under my bare feet. The food is crunchy with sand, the water muddy with sand and if I dare shed a tear, it leaves a print of my weakness against the sand on my cheek.'

ROSA: Where's that from?

SIBI: Oh, you don't think I could have thought that out for myself?

ROSA: Did you?

SIBI: No. That was from a letter from my father to me – written for a birthday of mine, years ago – in the days when he still could write. It's not that they stopped him from writing – he got sick . . .

ROSA: I was just going to say, they now even have a nice TV in their cells . . .

SIBI: In the beginning they never allowed him to write to anyone, but we found ways and means to get word from him. Then he got weaker and sicker and now they say he's dying. Of course, one learns not to believe anything in a brown envelope that comes from a private box in Pretoria, but in this case I'm willing to be proved wrong.

ROSA: They wouldn't joke about death.

SIBI: If I had to believe everything around me, I'd be as mad as you!

ROSA: I'm fine.

SIBI: Oh? In a prison like this, through choice? Sane? Fine?

ROSA: I'm a teacher.

SIBI: Of course. And what do you teach your kids? 'Boys and girls, behold the panorama, but don't look over your shoulders. Beyond those terrible walls are tortured people, angry people, hating people, who will one day come out and get you!' Do you teach that to your children, Rosa?

ROSA: The prison walls are ideal to practise tennis against and for ball games. I teach the kids about culture and beauty and hope and love and a good life.

SIBI: Then you are a great liar, schoolteacher. And a fool.

(KARIN *enters with a tray*.)

KARIN: Here's the tea. Now what happens? I also want tea. Must I now go and sit in the kitchen because of the rules?

SIBI: No, I'll go, I'm used to kitchens. They should come for me soon. I'd actually like to freshen up. Do you have a maid's quarters?

ROSA: No, we do our own housework.

SIBI: So where do I sleep?

ROSA: In Karin's room.

KARIN: No, Rosa! It's in such a terrible mess . . .

ROSA: Then she can clean it. Hey, Sibi? Make yourself useful until you're fetched.

SIBI: (to KARIN) Yes, I take milk. One sugar?

(KARIN *hesitates, then has to serve her. She stirs in the sugar and hands* SIBI *the cup.*)

SIBI: Thanks.

(*She exits.*)

KARIN: Why are you fighting with her? She's one of them, Rosa, take care!

ROSA: One of them? Who's them?

KARIN: Those terrorists – communists – anti-whites – blacks . . . oh, I don't know. I just know she wants to harm us. Everything we love and care about, she hates. She'll destroy our lives. Don't even answer her back, just say 'yes' and 'no' and let's get it over with. Please, Rosa, I'm so scared.

ROSA: Well, I'm not scared! I stand aside for no one, black or otherwise!

(KARIN *peers down the corridor.* ROSA *pours a drink.*)

KARIN: Should I give her clean sheets?

ROSA: What have you got that she might catch?

KARIN: Be serious! I just thought she . . . oh God, I didn't make space for her in my cupboard . . .

ROSA: I'm going to get those bastards at the office for this! I'm sure that baboon Grobbelaar had a finger in this little pie. 'Let's put the Kaffir in with the schoolteachers and see what happens!' Sibi Magala.

KARIN: Who?

ROSA: Madam in there. Sibi Magala or something . . .

KARIN: Magala?

ROSA: Sibi . . . like C.B.

KARIN: Magala . . . Makhale?

ROSA: That's it, Makhala.

KARIN: Makhale! She must be the daughter of Alfred Makhale! Oh God, I won't have her here in my house . . .

ROSA: You know this Alfred Makhala?
KARIN: Makhale! Remember, when I came here and met you and told you about him and you said it was OK, he was probably over at Pollsmore Prison with Nelson Mandela and the others. Remember, Rosa, I told you all about him. They say he helped plant that bomb in 1968. Seven people killed. My uncle lost a leg!
ROSA: Yes, but...
KARIN: I didn't know he was still here...
ROSA: He doesn't sound very important to me.
KARIN: Alfred Makhale. My parents talked about him. Even our dog's name was Makhale! My uncle had to stop working after that; I mean, what could he do with only one leg? Then he died. And all the time this murderer is just round the corner from me...
ROSA: Karin, he's in a maximum-security prison! He's not windsurfing outside!
KARIN: I won't have that girl in my room. It *is* my room!
ROSA: But he's dying...
KARIN: His daughter is here. I'm sure she's involved too. They all are!
ROSA: And I always thought you never got involved in politics.
KARIN: This is not politics, this is death! Oh God, it all comes back to me, all that whispering about him, all that fear. I swore I'd never listen to it again. And now they're here in my house, in my bed... I won't... I won't...
(*She cries.* ROSA *is helpless.*)
ROSA: But he's dying...
KARIN: Nobody can force me. I'll resign if I must. I won't be forced to be friendly!
ROSA: Well, for your information, I'm not going to resign. I like my job and my life here and I'm certainly not going to throw all that up because of having to play Kaffir-nanny for twenty-four hours.
KARIN: But my room...
ROSA: So play ball, Karin, because things will be back to normal tomorrow and we have to live together happily ever after

while she throws bombs and stones on the mainland!

KARIN: No one can force me!

ROSA: Oh?

(*She twists* KARIN's *arm painfully.*)

I'm not going to lose everything because of some cocky little black bitch, do you understand?

KARIN: Ow, Rosa . . . please don't . . . ow . . .

ROSA: Do you understand!

KARIN: Yes . . . yes . . . yes . . .

(*A knock at the door.* ROSA *lets her go.* KARIN *pulls away, frightened.* ROSA *is suddenly horrified at what has happened.*)

GROBBELAAR: (*Off*) Miss Rosa? It's me – Grobbelaar!

ROSA: I'll kill him . . .

GROBBELAAR: (*Off*) How many of you are in there?

KARIN: Two . . .

GROBBELAAR: (*Off*) Then I can't come in!

ROSA: It's two whites only!

GROBBELAAR: (*Off*) Then I'm coming in!

(*He enters.*)

GROBBELAAR: I'm here for the Kaffir girl.

KARIN: You've found a place for her? Thank God . . .

GROBBELAAR: No, Miss Karin, to see her father. What's wrong with your arm?

KARIN: Er . . . nothing.

ROSA: She's in Karin's room, Grobbelaar.

GROBBELAAR: Oh.

KARIN: She's in *my* room, Grobbelaar!

ROSA: It was you, wasn't it?

GROBBELAAR: Hey?

ROSA: You suggested that we take her in!

GROBBELAAR: No, I don't make those sort of decisions. They are made from the top. They'll be grateful. You'll see, Miss Rosa, they'll make a special effort for you two now.

KARIN: Did you know she was the daughter of Alfred Makhale?

GROBBELAAR: They all sound the same to me.

ROSA: Oh, never mind! Just take her away, Grobbelaar, it's already been a far too exciting day for these two spinster ladies.

GROBBELAAR: Don't have to be, you know, miss.
ROSA: Be what?
GROBBELAAR: A spinster, miss.
ROSA: Thank you, Grobbelaar.
KARIN: Grobbelaar, please don't go ...
ROSA: But isn't this your day off?
GROBBELAAR: Yes, Miss Rosa.
ROSA: Then why are you working?
GROBBELAAR: No, I thought you might need me around today, what with the Kaffir girl and everything.
ROSA: Thank you, Grobbelaar.
KARIN: Thanks, Grobbelaar.

(SIBI *enters wearing a colourful ethnic kaftan.*)

GROBBELAAR: I've come for you, hurry up!
KARIN: Hell's bells, now there are four of us in the same room!
SIBI: Don't worry, I won't tell the boss.
GROBBELAAR: OK, Miss Rosa, Miss Karin. (*Gruffly to* SIBI) Get a move on, man, we're late!
SIBI: Just leave the key under the mat. I promise I won't bring back strange men.

(*She exits after* GROBBELAAR.)

KARIN: You see, she's making fun of us!
ROSA: Forget about her, Karin. Here, I'll pour you a nice drink. Relax!
KARIN: Hell's bells ... no, really, I shouldn't ...

(*But* ROSA *pours her a stiff drink, which she accepts. She then peers off to her room.*)

KARIN: Do you think my room is OK?
ROSA: Here.

(*She tops up* KARIN'*s drink.*)

KARIN: That's why I didn't want to come to this place with its walls and cells and horrible secrets. They frighten me more than anything in the world. I want children one day, Rosa, if I find the right man, but I can't with them waiting to kill my babies. And then I came here – remember, on the same boat as you? – and got trapped by seasickness ... and now ... I'm not also going to lose everything, Rosa, I swear!

ROSA: We'll both look back on this in a few days and laugh, you watch what I tell you. Change the subject.

KARIN: I'm not also going to lose everything, Rosa!

ROSA: Change the subject!

KARIN: To what?

ROSA: I said change the subject – talk about anything else!
(*Pause.*)

KARIN: Rosa?

ROSA: *Ja?*

KARIN: Have you slept with your friend from Jo'burg?
(ROSA *stares at her amazed.*)

ROSA: What on earth made you ask that?

KARIN: I don't know...

ROSA: You've never asked me something like that before, Karin.

KARIN: I just... well, earlier on I was talking to Grobbelaar about children and marriage and... suddenly I just wondered... you know...

ROSA: I don't have to tell you things like that!

KARIN: But you said...

ROSA: I said change the subject – don't make conversation!
(*Pause.*)

KARIN: I lived with a man once. Well, not quite, he was still a boy. No, it's true... a Rhodesian chap... he was in college with me, and for one holiday we decided to share a place, you know, to see how it would be. Cheaper for two, you know...

ROSA: You never told me!
(*She laughs.*)

KARIN: Sounds so silly. It wasn't a laughing matter then. I had to sneak my things out so my parents wouldn't know and stop me. He also. He lived with his widowed ma. Well... anyway, when the holidays were over, he went back to his ma and I stayed on.

ROSA: And?

KARIN: *Ja*, maybe he missed home cooking and... I don't know ... maybe we knew each other too well, because nothing ever happened, you know, like that. I can't say I liked it. Living with a man. It's off-putting seeing his things all over the place

          – socks and underpants and his toothpaste-tube all squeezed and the cap never on it – and he never washed the bath, and he used to . . .
          (*Pause.*)

ROSA: What? Come on, you must tell me!
KARIN: (*Whispers*) *Poep.*
ROSA: What?
          (KARIN *starts laughing.*)
KARIN: Fart! *Poep*! You know? Even though he closed the door to his room every night, I'd hear them – like thunder!
          (*She demonstrates the* poeps. *They both fall about laughing.* ROSA *takes up the noises. It is a welcome release.*)
ROSA: No wonder you hate this place!
KARIN: Hey?
ROSA: The wind!
          (*More laughter. But* KARIN *is slowly going over to tears.* ROSA *holds forth.*)
ROSA: Well, I'm afraid I've never had any experience like that. I'm sure my one never does that sort of thing. He's too English – they never *poep*.
          (*She laughs, then notices* KARIN *huddled.*)
ROSA: Hey, what's wrong?
KARIN: Just listen to me. Here I sit, nostalgic about something that hasn't even happened to me, and all I really have on this forgotten rock in the sea is the reality of Grobbelaar and my colour poster of the Springbok Rugby Team!
ROSA: *Ja, ja*, you're quite safe with the Springboks. We'll donate Grobbelaar to the SPCA. Come now, stop crying.
KARIN: Don't cry over spilt milk?
ROSA: That's right.
KARIN: That just makes it worse!
          (*She cries.*)
ROSA: Karin. Listen, man, it's really terribly overrated, all this talk of sex and that sort of thing. Yes, I've slept with my man from Jo'burg. A few times. It keeps him happy to be so plunged in guilt that he can't wait for the next time. But it's really nothing to write home about.

KARIN: Then why's everybody doing it?

ROSA: Because waterskiing's too difficult. Come on, sit up. Look at the panorama. Just think of all the millions of eyes looking across at the island and wondering what strange things are happening here tonight. And if only they knew. (*She stands in front of the window and 'exposes' herself to the view.*) Look, you randy bastards! First one across the water gets a cookie!

(KARIN *is horrified.*)

ROSA: Here, you chauvinist pigs! A meat pie and two cream puffs for the first one with the guts to leave his mummy.

(*Then* KARIN *jumps up with a shriek of delight and does it too.*)

KARIN: Go for it!

(*She 'exposes' herself. There is a loud commotion outside.*)

KARIN: Oh, hell's bells, someone saw me!

SIBI: (*Off*) No, don't you make excuses, you pig! Don't you dare point a finger at my father, you white piece of rubbish!

(SIBI *enters with* GROBBELAAR.)

GROBBELAAR: Rubbish? You just listen here . . .

SIBI: I don't listen to murderers and killers of children. Fuck off!

GROBBELAAR: Jisis, nobody talks to me like this!

SIBI: Then start getting used to it, Whitey!

GROBBELAAR: I'm not going to take this from a Kaffir, Miss Rosa . . .

ROSA: Calm down, both of you . . .

SIBI: And don't you come with your 'calm down' crap! Just stand away from me, all of you. OK?

ROSA: I said calm down!

KARIN: Rosa, there are four of us . . .

ROSA: What?

KARIN: One, two, three, four . . .

ROSA: Then you two get out!

KARIN: I'll go. It's OK, I'll go. And Grobbelaar too. Grobbelaar, come . . .

GROBBELAAR: She's an animal. Like all the others – I warn you . . . (*He sneers at* SIBI.) *Ja*, and you people want to run this land? Listen, necklacing is too good for you. They should chain people like you to the walls of the city and let the seagulls peck out your eyes, like in the Bible!

SIBI: Wonderful idea. I'll make a note of it in my book of lists and reserve that one specially for you, you racist pig!

(GROBBELAAR *is about to grab her.*)

KARIN: (*Screams*) Grobbelaar!

(*She hangs on to him and forces him to leave the room with her.*)

GROBBELAAR: Fucking Kaffir bitch...

(*They exit.* SIBI *sits with her hands covering her face.* ROSA *is visibly rattled.*)

ROSA: You've got a damn cheek, causing a riot in my house. I think you owe me some explanation.

SIBI: I owe you nothing.

ROSA: An explanation.

SIBI: Nothing, Whitey!

(*She gives* ROSA *an F.U. sign.*)

ROSA: Now listen carefully to me, comrade. This is my house and you owe me some respect and manners, not because I'm your white madam, but because you're my guest, whether we like it or not! So pack away your 'radical chic', because here we do things my way, and my way is soft and civilized and do you hear me loud and clear? Hey? You haven't got a hope, Sibi! I'll just call the authorities and you'll be dead — because I'm white and I'm right. OK?

SIBI: OK.

ROSA: Calm?

SIBI: I said OK. I want a drink.

ROSA: Please?

SIBI: Please!

ROSA: I've only got whisky and cherry brandy.

SIBI: Soda-water. I don't drink.

ROSA: Oh, the purity of *amandla*. You don't drink, you don't smoke and you don't smile — what do you do? Do you fart?

SIBI: What?

ROSA: *Poep*, you know... phhhhhhhhhhhhh!

(SIBI *suddenly laughs.*)

ROSA: Ah, good morning, sunshine.

SIBI: Jesus, you people ... *poep*?

ROSA: Never mind, it was a means to an end. OK, soda-water. Sorry, no ice. It's in the fridge and I don't intend leaving you alone for one moment.

SIBI: In case I do what?

ROSA: In case you run away and then I'll never know your terrible secrets. Here. Say thank you?

SIBI: Thank you.

ROSA: That's better. (*Pause. She sits down.*) So, talk to me.

SIBI: Nice view.

ROSA: What was all that shouting about?

SIBI: He insulted my father.

ROSA: He was provoking you.

SIBI: I won't take shit from any man, especially not a Boer!

ROSA: I'll drink to that. Anyway, Grobbelaar's not a Boer: he's covered in fur and listens to the police radio in stereo by sticking two bananas in his ears. So, how's your father?

SIBI: They told the truth for once. He looked terrible.

ROSA: Yes, but admit one thing: in spite of what he did, we look after him. You saw for yourself.

SIBI: You people can't afford to take chances with black political prisoners, not after Biko.

ROSA: Was he conscious?

SIBI: You mean, did he see me? No. But I really wanted to sit with him tonight, just to be with him. It's been many years since I saw him. But they pushed me out, very politely, so as not to make any bruises.

ROSA: You can always go back tomorrow.

SIBI: My twenty-four hours is over at noon.

ROSA: Where must you go back to?

SIBI: Listen, leave me alone! Don't try and change the subject! I've got nothing to tell you, white teacher. That old man was a strong, healthy father and now look what you've done to him, so get off my back. I won't lie down so easily!

ROSA: Don't blame me for your star status! If you people want to rock the boat, then expect to get splashed and don't moan when you get wet! Right. The programme is as follows: we watch the early TV news to see what's happening over there in the real world and then we have supper. It's fish night tonight. You're very welcome to join us. Then we prepare classes and read and talk. That's how we relax. Any questions? (*Pause. Then eventually*)

SIBI: Do you have a husband?

ROSA: A boyfriend, but he's not here.

SIBI: Ah, not one of the staff from the prison, then?

ROSA: Like hell. He's in Jo'burg.

SIBI: Jo'burg. I grew up there. What's it like nowadays? They say it's a war zone.

ROSA: I really wouldn't know. So you like fish?

SIBI: It's funny how after a time even the horrible things become romantic and you miss them. The train to Jo'burg from Soweto; location life; raids; the laughter; it's very quiet in the Free State. When you watch the sunset or look out in the streets there, all you see is nothing. You feel like the last human left. (*Pause.*) Yes, I like fish. So you're going to marry a man from Jo'burg and get a house with a garden and electricity and running water and a car and go to church every Sunday and show him photos of this place and remember the hot sun and the high tides and building sandcastles with the children between the barbed wire. Your friend tells me they used stone from the quarry here to build the Cape Town castle. Now that I really didn't know.

ROSA: Yes.

SIBI: Amazing. Now that's a really important bit of information. You know I'm having a wonderful time. You're a very good hostess, Rosa, my dear – soft and civilized and in a world so far from mine I can scarcely hear the sound of your voice . . . (*She stops and seems to stumble.*)

ROSA: What is it?

SIBI: Nothing . . . I need fresh air. If it's not against the law, I'd like to go out. It's not every day that someone like me gets a chance to walk around outside the fences.

ROSA: It's probably also against the rules. For someone like you.

SIBI: You enjoy having me here, don't you? Makes you feel you're living in danger, but without guilt or risk.

ROSA: I suppose it's different . . .
   (KARIN *calls from within.*)
KARIN: Oh no, man, I also want to come in now. Grobbelaar and I are all talked out. Someone else must go now!
SIBI: Let me go for a walk. (*Calls*) It's OK. I'm going.
   (KARIN *peeps round the door.*)
KARIN: And what are we going to do at supper? We're not allowed to sit around the table together. I mean, who eats in the kitchen?
ROSA: I'll give you three guesses.
   (GROBBELAAR *enters.*)
GROBBELAAR: You're supposed to stay right here till we fetch you tomorrow.
SIBI: So stop me. Go on, take out your gun or whatever and beat me over the head.
ROSA: You make yourself quite irresistible.
GROBBELAAR: If you let her walk about a restricted area, Miss Rosa, I'll have to put in a report.
KARIN: Please decide now!
SIBI: But why don't you come with me, Mr Grobbelaar? Surely I couldn't have a better alibi, and you a more talkative companion. I might even race you down to the beach, where we can play blind-man's-buff, or kick-the-Kaffir, or what's new around your playpen.
KARIN: Stop it, please. It's bad enough as it is, without you going on like this. Rosa, please, you tell them.
ROSA: Grobbelaar?
GROBBELAAR: Miss Rosa?
ROSA: Miss Makhale wants to go for a walk. Will you just stay with her so that there's no trouble?
GROBBELAAR: No way, Miss Rosa, that's not part of my orders.
ROSA: No, it's me asking. Please?
GROBBELAAR: Just as a favour to you, Miss Rosa.
ROSA: Thank you, Grobbelaar.
GROBBELAAR: You owe me one. Come.
   (*He exits.*)
SIBI: I promise – he says one word to me about my father, I'll take a stone and smash his face.

(*She exits.* ROSA *gives a deep sigh.*)

ROSA: Shit, I need a drink!

KARIN: Hell's bells, no, I shouldn't . . .

(ROSA *pours them a drink*. KARIN *peers outside*.)

KARIN: Was it OK for us to let her go with him? Maybe I should've gone along . . . oh no, then there would be three . . .

ROSA: 'Ten little Kaffir kids running from the law. The corporal opened fire and then there were four.' What a madhouse . . . have you ever thought that maybe someone somewhere thinks we're all as crazy as these seagulls? Hell, please – 'no more than one person in a room at the same time'. . .

KARIN: It's the law, Rosa.

ROSA: And just because suddenly that law affects us, we realize what a load of mindless lunacy it is? So what about the other laws that protect us, hey? Karin? You know more about politics than me, what about the other laws?

KARIN: If there were no laws, there would be chaos. It would be every man for himself. We'd have riots. We'd be fighting for our survival!

ROSA: Isn't that the story of our lives?

(*She also peers outside*.)

ROSA: What are they doing down there . . . ?

KARIN: I don't think we should've let her go with Grobbelaar . . .

ROSA: Oh, come on, Grobbelaar's harmless. And anyway, what do you think he'd do to her here?

KARIN: She's black. She's his target. He's her mortal enemy! There's no difference to them between one white face and another. We all look alike to them.

ROSA: Where did you hear that? Who told you that?

KARIN: Many people . . . actually, my Aunt Gracie.

ROSA: Do I look like you? Or Grobbelaar?

KARIN: No . . .

(*She giggles.*)

ROSA: Let's get supper together.

KARIN: We'd better take out the good plates.

ROSA: What the hell for? It's nobody's birthday.

KARIN: I don't want her to think we're giving her food on our old set. I don't want her to think we're treating her like a black.

ROSA: But she is a black!

KARIN: Come on, man, you know what I mean! In our kitchen at home we always had some tin plates and tin mugs for the garden boy and the maid and whoever came to do some work. It was always like that.

ROSA: We haven't got tin mugs and plates.

KARIN: That's what I mean, she might think we're hiding them ...

ROSA: This is a madhouse! Karin, we eat off these plates every day. We – you and me! Now she will also have a chance. *Our* plates! OK? We can always break her plate on the rocks when she's finished, if it'll make you happy.

KARIN: But the good plates ...

ROSA: The good plates stay locked up for an occasion, like always. This is not an occasion.

KARIN: No, but I just thought ...

ROSA: Yes, well, Karin, leave all that to me. I know how to handle this situation. OK?

(*Pause.*)

KARIN: OK.

ROSA: Just tell me something. At your house, you know, with the tin plates and mugs? Your dog ... Makhale?

KARIN: No, four dogs – Makhale was a Rottweiler, then Smuts, Doris and Henry.

ROSA: Didn't their tin plates get mixed up with the garden boys' tin plates?

KARIN: No, the dogs ate out of their own nice dishes with their names on them, and even, sometimes, from *my* plate. My father would get so cross ... oh no!

(*During this* GROBBELAAR *enters carrying a motionless* SIBI.)

ROSA: Oh God ...

GROBBELAAR: No, really, Miss Rosa, I don't know what happened ...

ROSA: What happened?

GROBBELAAR: I really don't know ... we were just walking down there by the rocks, me behind her – but not close – when she ... I don't know ...

ROSA: I don't believe it ...

KARIN: What? Is she dead?
ROSA: You killed her?
KARIN: What!
GROBBELAAR: No, Miss Rosa, man, I swear she just fell . . .
KARIN: Oh dear God, is she really dead?
ROSA: Dead?
GROBBELAAR: Miss Rosa, I'm telling you . . .
KARIN: Put her down!
ROSA: Karin, don't go!
KARIN: I want to get a blanket . . . anyway, we're four!
ROSA: But if she's dead, that law doesn't count!
   (GROBBELAAR *puts* SIBI *down on the couch.*)
GROBBELAAR: Miss Rosa, all I can say is . .
KARIN: Hell's bells, Grobbelaar, did you shoot her? I can't believe it!
GROBBELAAR: Miss Karin, man . . .
ROSA: I knew we shouldn't have let her go with him. It's just a way of life now, murdering babies, raping women . . .
   (*She stops, horrified by what she has said.*)
GROBBELAAR: OK, Miss Rosa, OK. I will remember all you just said to me. For ever I'll remember!
   (*He exits.* KARIN *runs after him.*)
KARIN: No, wait, Grobbelaar, you can't leave her like this!
ROSA: I've walked with him alone at night on the beach. There but for the grace of God lie I . . .
KARIN: It's just too terrible . . . what are we going to do? Rosa, we must contact the police . . . oh no, he is the police . . . Rosa? What are we going to do?
ROSA: Er . . . you did First Aid?
KARIN: No. Never.
ROSA: What about your bloody diploma from college! You always said you were the best in the class!
KARIN: Yes, but I never learnt anything.
ROSA: Then feel for her pulse.
KARIN: Maybe you should . . .
ROSA: I don't know where her pulse is!
KARIN: It's here, man, same as us.
ROSA: Go on, Karin, she won't bite you!

(*Pause.*)

KARIN: Do you think he raped her?

ROSA: What do you think?

KARIN: There've been so many cases like this . . .

ROSA: Oh God . . .

KARIN: There's no blood . . . oh, hell's bells, our new sofa! Can you see blood?

ROSA: But I didn't hear a shot, did you?

KARIN: No . . .

ROSA: Look at her neck, maybe he strangled her.

KARIN: Do you think so? I can't see anything from here . . .

(*Pause.*)

KARIN: Rosa, with a dead body in our house . . . I mean, they won't think we did it, hey?

ROSA: Don't be ridiculous! Grobbelaar was with her!

KARIN: Yes, but what if he says he wasn't? It's his word against ours.

ROSA: He did it!

KARIN: Ja, but what if he says he didn't? They'll believe him – they stick together, the police. They'll say we did it! You said to them I didn't want her here!

(*She starts crying.*)

ROSA: Oh shit! Well, she can't lie here. Help me carry her into the kitchen.

KARIN: But she's dead!

ROSA: I don't expect her to cook the supper! Take her legs, Karin, for God's sake, don't make me angry!

(*They tentatively pick up* SIBI.)

ROSA: She weighs a ton . . .

KARIN: Dead people do. Oh, hell's bells . . .

ROSA: Is the sofa ruined?

KARIN: I see no blood . . . maybe she had a heart attack . . .

ROSA: Hey?

KARIN: If there's no blood . . .

ROSA: Anyone who sees Grobbelaar coming at them in a state of *sexualis erectus* is bound to have a heart attack . . .

(*She starts laughing. The more she tries to stop, the more she laughs.* KARIN *is shocked.*)

KARIN: Rosa! How can you make a terrible joke like that!
ROSA: I'm sorry . . . I'm sorry . . .
(*They lift* SIBI *again. Then* ROSA *starts giggling.*)
ROSA: We might have to bury her in the garden after dark.
KARIN: Rosa!
ROSA: . . . near where we want the bougainvillaea!
(ROSA *collapses in hysterics.* KARIN *struggles with* SIBI's *weight. We see* SIBI *pull* KARIN's *hair hard.*)
KARIN: Ow, Rosa, that was sore!
ROSA: I'm sorry . . . I'll try and stop . . .
(*But she can't.* SIBI *pulls* KARIN's *hair again.*)
KARIN: Ow, hell, man, that's not funny, Rosa!
ROSA: But I'm not doing anything.
(*Then* SIBI *gives a loud, long* poep *sound.* KARIN *screams. They drop the 'body'.* SIBI *is helpless with laughter.*)
SIBI: Oh my God, you're funny . . .
(ROSA *and* KARIN *can't believe their eyes.*)
SIBI: I must've hit my head when I fell out there. I fainted. OK? It happens quite often.
KARIN: You're alive!
ROSA: We thought you were dead!
SIBI: No, actually, I'm pregnant.
KARIN: No wonder you were so heavy.
ROSA: Pregnant?
SIBI: I fainted. I'm hungry. And at this moment I have this craving for chocolate cake and beer!
ROSA: Bloody pregnant?
KARIN: You're alive, thank God!
(*She embraces* SIBI *impulsively.*)
SIBI: Now, will one of you two white bitches get me something to eat or do I phone *The New York Times*!

END OF ACT ONE

Act Two

―――――― o ――――――

The lights go up on ROSA *at the table, stacking the soup plates.* SIBI *enters carrying a covered bowl, which holds the fish cakes.* ROSA *hands her the stacked soup plates.*

SIBI: Nice plates. You brought out the china specially for me?

ROSA: From the Indian market.

SIBI: Close enough.

    (*She exits with the plates.* ROSA *serves for all three.* KARIN *appears, looks around, then approaches the table and sits.*)

KARIN: There wasn't enough salt in the soup.

ROSA: It was fine.

KARIN: No, not enough salt . . .

    (SIBI *enters and sits.* KARIN *looks from one to the other, waiting, then gets up and exits. She sits calmly outside in the passage.*)

ROSA: Eat, before it gets cold.

SIBI: There was too much salt in the soup.

ROSA: Shut up and eat, Sibi!

    (*They eat.*)

KARIN: (*Off*) Do you want tomato sauce with the fish cakes?

SIBI: That would be nice.

ROSA: Good. It's in the kitchen.

    (SIBI *mutters in Xhosa and exits.* KARIN *enters and scuttles towards the table.*)

KARIN: This is ridiculous! Where do I eat?

ROSA: Eat!

KARIN: (*Sitting*) I'm so hungry.

    (*She starts eating as* SIBI *enters with the tomato sauce and sits.*)

KARIN: Oh no . . .

(She gets up.)

ROSA: Will you stop behaving like an idiot!

KARIN: Rosa...

ROSA: Sit and eat your fucking food!

KARIN: But it's against the law.

SIBI: No, no – it *is* the law.
  (She waits for KARIN *to sit and nearly takes a mouthful before she says)*
  'No more than one person at a time.'

KARIN: I'm not hungry.
  (She gets up, gives her plate a last, longing look and exits to her place in the passage.)

SIBI: Nice food.

ROSA: Not too much 'salt'?

SIBI: It's fish, what can I tell you.

ROSA: Karin? Sibi likes your food.
  (Pause.)

KARIN: *(Off)* Oh.

SIBI: Especially the fish cakes...

ROSA: Karin? Especially your fish cakes.

KARIN: *(Off)* There was too much salt in the soup.

SIBI: No, no...

KARIN: *(Off)* Never mind, I heard you.

SIBI: I don't mind salt really... *(To* ROSA*)* I'm sorry, I didn't mean to upset her. *(Calls)* I really liked the soup!

KARIN: *(Off)* Yes, thank you.

ROSA: Karin?

KARIN: Yes, Rosa!

ROSA: It'll be cold if you don't come now.

KARIN: *(Off)* Never mind.
  (Pause.)

ROSA: What are you doing?

KARIN: *(Off)* I'm waiting for one of you to leave.

ROSA: We're not going anywhere.
  (Pause as they eat. Then SIBI *gets up.)*

SIBI: I'll go...

ROSA: Stay! She must grow up.

SIBI: Yes, she's hungry.
> (*She takes* KARIN's *plate and exits to the passage.*)

KARIN: (*Off*) Yes, I'm hungry!

SIBI: (*Off*) Here.

KARIN: (*Off*) Thanks.

SIBI: (*Off*) You go back in.

KARIN: (*Off*) No, I'm all right here. Really, it's lovely here.

ROSA: Will you two come and sit down before I really get cross?
> (SIBI *enters.*)

SIBI: I'll clear up the kitchen.

KARIN: (*Off*) We don't expect you to . . .

ROSA: Karin!
> (KARIN *enters holding her plate.*)

KARIN: All right, Rosa, count now – one, two, three . . .

ROSA: I'm going – to get the pudding ready. Sit!
> (ROSA *exits.* KARIN *sits.*)

KARIN: We don't have pudding. What pudding? Did you ask for pudding?

SIBI: No.

KARIN: Good heavens, what could it be? (*Looks down at her plate*) Now it's all cold.

SIBI: Make a hamburger out of it.

KARIN: A fishburger – it's fish.

SIBI: A fishcakehamburger!

KARIN: (*Giggles*) Sounds so funny – a fishcakehamburger.

SIBI: Nice recipe.

KARIN: Yes, it's my favourite. It's also so simple.

SIBI: Surrounded by all the fish, all you need is the cake.

KARIN: Hey?

SIBI: Eat, Karin.
> (KARIN *eats. Chews. A fish-bone. She pretends it's not there.*)

SIBI: Don't swallow the fish-bone, Karin.

KARIN: Mmmmmmm?

SIBI: Spit it out.

KARIN: Eh . . . (*Through clenched teeth*) No fish-bone . . .

SIBI: I had an old aunt in Port Elizabeth who swallowed a fish-bone and died!

(KARIN *immediately spits the bone into the palm of her hand.*)

SIBI: Put it on the plate.

KARIN: No, it's OK.

SIBI: You're going to sit all night with a fish-bone in your hand?

KARIN: There are no fish-bones in my fish cakes!

SIBI: No?

KARIN: No!

(*She takes another forkful – and finds another fish-bone.*)

SIBI: And what's that? A submarine?

(*She laughs.* ROSA *enters with three small bowls of ice-cream. During this scene the wind has come up and can be heard constantly in the background from now to the end of the play.*)

ROSA: The wind's coming up.

KARIN: Mmmmmmmmm.

ROSA: What's wrong with you?

SIBI: Fish-bone.

ROSA: Spit it out, Karin. I had an aunt who swallowed a fish-bone and died.

SIBI: Really?

(KARIN *removes the bone and gets up stiffly. Takes her tape recorder and sits on the couch.*)

KARIN: I don't feel like any pudding . . . hello? Testing one, two, one, two . . .

ROSA: Must you always do that?

KARIN: I have to check if it's working. I don't want to talk out everything and then find that nothing makes sense!

ROSA: True.

KARIN: Hello, Mummy, it's me again, Karin. Listen, it's now the evening of the same day that I spoke to Mummy earlier. It's now . . .

ROSA: After supper.

KARIN: . . . after supper.

SIBI: We had lovely fish cakes . . .

KARIN: We had lovely fish cakes . . . shhh, Sibi! . . . Oh, Mummy, listen to Rosa making jokes again. Anyway, I don't know if you can hear, but the South-easter wind's blowing up a storm as usual. Mummy, remember you always found our South-easter so exciting and healthy because it supposedly blows away all the pollution, but this wind can also make people go mad ...

(ROSA *and* SIBI *exchange glances*.)

I can tell you, it makes the kids at school impossible ... er, what more can I say ... Oh, Mummy, today we had a bit of excitement. Today we had a visitor ... (*She stops the machine*.) This is ridiculous! I won't carry on with this pretending!

ROSA: That's what I said to the copshop, but our lives must carry on in spite of 'interruptions'. We've had supper. Now we prepare classes and read. Carry on with your tape to your ma.

KARIN: It can wait till tomorrow.

ROSA: You owe your ma a tape, Karin.

SIBI: Oh, please don't feel shy or think that I'm in the way, just in case you want to tell your ma there's a cheeky Kaffir girl in your bed.

KARIN: Shhhh, please! You promised not to say anything! They listen in.

ROSA: Oh, rubbish!

KARIN: Oh yes they do! They'll hear there are more than just two of us in this room. Please, I don't want trouble. And (*to* SIBI) we never used the word 'Kaffir' in our house. We grew up as Christians.

ROSA: Amen. Get on with your tape, Karin. It's just us two, remember? You and me.

SIBI: You and I.

KARIN: But I'm embarrassed.

ROSA: Then look the other way and pretend you're on your own.

(KARIN *gets her machine ready and starts again*.)

KARIN: Right, now where was I?

SIBI: The visitor from outer space.

ROSA: Shhhh!

KARIN: Mummy, as I said, today we had a visitor. She's from ... from the North. She's come to visit her father. Shame, he's quite sick. She's ... er ... pregnant ...

(*She stops. Exits weeping.* SIBI *gets up to follow her.*)

ROSA: Leave her. She can't express herself. Let her cry.

SIBI: She's a teacher, for God's sake. If she can't express herself, what can she do?

ROSA: She recites and teaches others what she learnt parrot-fashion from someone else who learnt it blindly from someone else who made it up! She's a good teacher.

SIBI: Sounds like 'Bantu Education'.

ROSA: Mmmm. I had a good teacher when I was at school. I was one of the lucky ones, hey? She wasn't good at her subject – chemistry or something – but she took an interest in me, took me out in civvies to art galleries and even the ballet once; but it wasn't just that: it was being treated like a grown-up that made all the difference. She would listen to my point of view, for what it was worth. She didn't laugh at me – well, at least, not to my face. She said that teaching was her life. Funny, since I started teaching here my life seems to have stopped.

SIBI: What did you really want to do?

(SIBI *sits down with* ROSA *and takes out of her bag a small baby-jacket that she is crocheting.*)

ROSA: I wanted to be an athlete. I ran well once, can you believe it? But in those days athletics wasn't a career, it was a hobby. OK. So I did what everyone else was told to do: I got something to fall back on. My diploma. Funny what a difference it makes, hey? Something to fall *back* on! No one ever said to me, get something to fall *forward* on! Always the retreat mentality, the negative. 'Rosa, get something to fall back on, because no matter what you want to do with your dream, it will be a flop!' So look at me now.

SIBI: A good job, a nice house, a faithful friend – and you're white. What more do you want?

ROSA: Oh, please, I wanted so much more in the beginning! I had such big dreams! I can't remember them all now, but they kept me awake so many nights and made me feel so brave and important. What were your dreams?

SIBI: You talking to me?

ROSA: Who else?

SIBI: I don't know. I'm asking: are you making polite conversation because the bosses in the copshop are listening in, and if you

play their game, you'll get a gold star in your homework book?
ROSA: Nobody listens in to me.
SIBI: You mean you're not even bugged?
ROSA: They're not interested.
SIBI: Shame. Dreams? I don't know. We blacks all have one dream, and after that, all little dreams are silly.
ROSA: Don't drag politics in, please!
SIBI: Everything is political: eating, houses, schools, God, love, sex, hate. Even the sun shines down to make your skin dark, while it bleaches our land white.
ROSA: You're here because of politics!
SIBI: Only after you people forced it on me! (*Pause.*) Yes, I also had dreams. Not to be a jogger like you; I don't even run from the riot police. No, I wanted to be a nurse, like my mother was before she was forced to give it up.
ROSA: You became a nurse?
SIBI: I planned and then fought with my mother, who wanted me to get a decent job and not work for whites ... oh yes, I once worked for whites to earn money to make my dream come true.
ROSA: Couldn't you get a bursary?
SIBI: Come on, teacher, we're talking about the years when it wasn't fashionable to sponsor a black face. Not with a father in jail and a mother in exile.
ROSA: You could've gone to the Press.
SIBI: The overseas Press had just discovered the Ayatollah ... So I spent my dream carrying letters from his lawyer to her lawyer, keeping their marriage alive with little messages, dodging police and informers. I inherited the burden of their revenge. I got involved. So here I am.
ROSA: Did you also throw bombs?
SIBI: That would be so simple, wouldn't it? No, I talked. I made speeches. I visited friends.
ROSA: Russia?
SIBI: Russia? What the hell is this white obsession with fucking Russia? Why must everything anti-apartheid come from Russia? Look, I've never been north of Jo'burg! You teach history?

ROSA: No, Karin does.
SIBI: Ah yes, the one who can't express herself. Listen, I talk a lot about a future because I know it will happen. You people seem to live happily in the past because it makes you feel strong.
ROSA: History is history.
SIBI: History is now! My father is history. You and I are history! And Karin teaches 'history'?
(*She indicates outside at the view.*)
ROSA: So . . . we all seem to have something in common.
(*The conversation seems to be over. Pause. Then* SIBI *starts laughing.*)
SIBI: Did you really think I was dead?
ROSA: Er . . . no . . . I don't know . . .
SIBI: You were very funny. (*Pause.*) Have you ever seen someone die?
ROSA: No, I looked away.
SIBI: But you were there?
ROSA: Yes, but I didn't want to see.
SIBI: Strange, with all the death that surrounds me every day, I have also never seen someone die. Yes, I've seen bodies; I've dressed bodies for the grave; I've carried bodies out of the streets; but never *that moment* when someone just vanishes in a breath. Like the wind that you can't see, suddenly it's gone . . . my father will be dead soon, oh yes, I know enough of the way dying people just lie there to be sure. Alone he will die, cross over without help.
ROSA: There are priests.
SIBI: I didn't mean he wanted his ID book stamped. I just want to be with him and hold his hand and touch him till he's gone on. It helps, they say.
ROSA: I wouldn't know. Oh, how morbid all this is. (*Shudders and gets up*) I want to be touched now, while I'm still alive, not just before I die, thank you very much! You don't drink?
SIBI: No, but go ahead.
ROSA: Hell, thanks. Whisky soda, no ice!
(SIBI *pours the drink while* ROSA *watches her carefully.*)
ROSA: I've never spoken to a black before.

SIBI: Long live apartheid ...
ROSA: No, I mean like a person ... I mean ... you know what I mean?
SIBI: You mean you've never spoken to a black before like you would talk to a white?
ROSA: I'd never say these things to a white!
SIBI: Then to who?
ROSA: 'To whom'! Anyway, don't be so cheeky. I just wanted to say that it's a change to talk to ... well, just to talk. You didn't have to talk to me, Sibi, you could've gone to bed.
SIBI: The History Teacher, I think, has claimed back her couch.
ROSA: We'll sort that out when you get tired. Are you tired?
SIBI: No.
ROSA: Doesn't the baby make you tired?
SIBI: Not yet.
ROSA: You don't look pregnant.
SIBI: That's good.
ROSA: How many months?
SIBI: They say eighteen weeks.
ROSA: Do you have any other kids?
SIBI: No.
ROSA: Your first?
SIBI: For a schoolteacher you ask the most intelligent questions.
ROSA: I'm trying to show my interest. I've never entertained a pregnant, black, banned, terrorist's daughter before.
SIBI: I appreciate your interest. Can we talk about your sex life now?
ROSA: Your husband? What does he do?
SIBI: Have you had any children?
ROSA: Don't be silly, I'm not married.
SIBI: Nor am I.
ROSA: Is that special? I thought all you blacks just had kids without ... er ...
SIBI: Without bothering to get married? I couldn't get married, because the man I fucked was already married, OK? I loved him. I wanted his child. I still do. I need a child. OK?
ROSA: OK, OK.

SIBI: I never really knew my father. He was arrested when I was very small. So I never knew a father at home. I've never walked with my father in the street. The few times I've seen him, we have to talk over the phone, looking through a glass window. I can't touch him. I can't tell him anything, because there are always warders, like – whatshisname? Your boyfriend?

ROSA: He's not my boyfriend!

SIBI: Like him – sitting on each side of the glass, listening. My baby will also maybe not know its father, but, like me, will come away strong when we talk of our struggle.

ROSA: Oh, blah, blah, blah! A baby needs a father, a man, real family warmth. The struggle, your politics, is cold. What have you got called Father? A photo from an overseas newspaper?

SIBI: I have a memory. Yes, I hope my father dies here soon. If they let him go free now, no one in the world will even recognize him. Alfred Makhale is strong in the dreams of many; my sick old father alone is my reality.

ROSA: But can you talk to him again tomorrow? Hold his hand?

SIBI: I don't know.

ROSA: You'll sit with him. There are some people around here who owe me some favours. What brutal rubbish! I'll make a plan.

SIBI: Do you really think you could –

(*But she stops short as* KARIN *enters in a dressing-gown, carrying her duvet and a framed photograph.*)

KARIN: I've brushed my teeth and my hair. Your bedroom is ready. I took everything I need.

ROSA: What's that in your hand?

KARIN: Just the picture of my parents. I always sleep with it next to my bed. It's good luck.

SIBI: That's nice. I'll go and prepare for bed. Oh, you won't mind if I put the picture of my parents next to the bed? You don't have to look at it. They're both banned people and their picture may not be seen. My secret. Good-night.

(*She exits.* KARIN *sits and covers herself with the duvet.*)

KARIN: Rosa, what is happening with us . . .

ROSA: Don't think about it, Karin, just look at the panorama.

(*They look out at the view.*)

KARIN: Rosa, what do we do about Grobbelaar?

ROSA: Hey?

KARIN: Those terrible things you said to him? You accused him of rape, even murder!

ROSA: No, I just thought she was dead ... so did you. I didn't say anything, really ... just shock.

KARIN: He'll never be the same towards us, Rosa. We've lost a friend.

ROSA: Grobbelaar was never a friend!

KARIN: He was my friend. You know, I've been thinking. I've been here so long, looking out at that view. I've never thought about the people back in there with no view.

ROSA: You mean Makhale.

KARIN: Imagine life here with no window, just the wind. Just the seagulls. Just the Grobbelaars. And maybe, once, a glimpse of us two white women playing with white children in the white sand, building sandcastles that the wind will blow back into the eyes of those watching us. I really want to leave here, Rosa. Please God, I must get that job.

ROSA: You will.

KARIN: No, I don't think I will. But I swear, if they turn me down again, I'd rather kill myself than stay here for ever, like now. (*She pulls herself together.*) Oh, I don't care ...

ROSA: I care.

KARIN: Then why did you say those terrible things to Grobbelaar? The only real friend we had? Just for the sake of a terrorist's daughter?

ROSA: There's much more to her than that, Karin. We talked.

KARIN: Talk? Oh, please, don't tell me about 'talk'! Don't tell me how suddenly you realize after ten minutes that she was a very nice girl in spite of everything.

ROSA: She's no fool.

KARIN: No, *I'm* the fool, she's in my bed! But that's all right, Rosa, I'll be the fool. I'll give her my bed, I'll give her supper and I'll give her clean sheets, but I will not talk to her and I will not listen to her and, oh God, I pray it's tomorrow and she's out of our lives.

(*She cries.* ROSA *is at a loss.*)

ROSA: Oh shit, why do you suddenly cry all the time? Stop crying all the time! You never cry! Are you sick?

KARIN: I'm frightened!

ROSA: Well, then ... take a pill and go to sleep. Here, take one of my special ones.

KARIN: No, I'm fine.

ROSA: Your nerves are getting on my nerves. Take the pill and settle down!

KARIN: Yes, but what will you do?

ROSA: I'm just going to check if the terrorist is comfortable and not wearing my best pyjamas. Karin, take the fucking pill and settle down!

KARIN: But will you be back?

ROSA: No, I'm running off to South America with Grobbelaar! Yes, I'll be back. I promise. I still need to prepare a lesson.

KARIN: This won't make me an addict, will it?

ROSA: If you don't take it, I might become one! It's only a pill ... shit ...

(*She exits with the supper dishes.* KARIN *studies the pill, then hides it under the couch. Picks up the tape recorder*)

KARIN: Dear Mummy ... don't be cross, but I just want to ask: why did you and Dad let me grow up so frightened? Too scared to be pretty, too terrified to talk back. I just always said 'I'm sorry'. About everything: 'sorry'. I never knew I could change things in my life. You made me so frightened that I'll never be free like her, and she's supposed to be banned! She laughs at me; they all laugh at me ... And if I killed myself, Mummy, would that really make any difference? Would I have to say 'I'm sorry' – because then there would be no one to send you postcards of the panorama? But I'm too frightened to commit suicide, just in case it would be the one thing I'd succeed in doing properly. I'm sorry, Mummy ...

(ROSA *enters with her briefcase. Sees* KARIN *is still awake and peers down at the tape recorder.*)

ROSA: It's not on 'record'.

KARIN: I know. I was just practising. (*She settles down.*) I think I'll just lie like this.

ROSA: With your slippers on, just in case something terrible happens and you have to run out with the furniture?

KARIN: No, I meant to take them off. Night, Rosa.

ROSA: Good-night, Karin.

(*Pause.* KARIN *pretends to settle down.* ROSA *takes a magazine out of her briefcase.*)

KARIN: What are you doing?

ROSA: Shut up and sleep, Karin. You've taken the pill?

KARIN: Yes, I have. Is that your grammar lesson for tomorrow?

ROSA: No, it's a magazine article on Robben Island. I want to write some things down to give to Sibi before she goes. My boyfriend sent it to me.

(*She takes her make-up off while reading from the magazine.* KARIN *listens, as she does throughout the rest of the scene, pretending to sleep in case one of them comes near her.*)

ROSA: 'When people speak of the island, it is usually with abhorrence. Its history does not read like a fairy-tale. Like a monster guarding the gateway to Africa, it has become a symbol of hopelessness, its reputation going back centuries. But this beautiful island does not deserve its ugly past, nor its offensive present. It is a forgotten paradise of teeming bird and marine life, probably the only stretch of totally unspoilt coast in southern Africa . . . it squats in the sea like a pimple on the face of the fairest cape in the whole circumference of the earth.' I love that bit.

(SIBI *enters.*)

SIBI: Bedtime story?

ROSA: I gave her a pill . . .

SIBI: Is she OK there?

ROSA: Look, let's just get this night over with, OK?

SIBI: OK. (*Reads*) 'South Africa's *Paradise Lost*'. I must remember to tell my father. (*Looks out at the view*) Funny, how liberal South African whites sat over there for years with this thorn in their eyes and carried on blindly sipping the good life.

ROSA: Say what you've come to say and go to bed. You'll wake Karin.

SIBI: Good-night. (*Pause.*) Rosa, you said I don't look pregnant.

ACT TWO

ROSA: No.
SIBI: Are you sure?
ROSA: What's your problem? You're going to have a baby. It's happened before. Relax.
SIBI: I'm scared my father will know.
ROSA: Sibi, your father's got other problems.
SIBI: I can't lie to him, you see, Rosa. I can't pretend. He's very strong. Very strict. He'll sense it. He'll demand to know. What can I tell him?
ROSA: You say, 'Pa, you're not losing a daughter, you're gaining a grandchild.'
SIBI: He'll ask who the father is.
ROSA: Tell him.
SIBI: Never.
ROSA: Come on, Sibi, was your married man really from outer space?
SIBI: Yes; he was white.
(*She exits.*)
ROSA: Karin? Are you awake?
(KARIN *pretends to sleep.* ROSA *checks and tucks her in.* GROBBELAAR *has been at the door, watching and listening.*)
ROSA: Karin? (*Sees* GROBBELAAR) Damn it, Grobbelaar, can't you knock?
GROBBELAAR: Didn't want to wake Miss Karin.
ROSA: I'm working.
GROBBELAAR: You never work this late, Miss Rosa.
ROSA: And will you stop calling me that?
GROBBELAAR: What must I call you?
ROSA: Anything you like, just leave us alone.
GROBBELAAR: Murderer?
ROSA: What?
GROBBELAAR: Like you called me anything you liked? Murderer? Rapist? What was the others?
ROSA: We thought she was dead, Grobbelaar.
GROBBELAAR: And that I did it?
ROSA: What do you expect us to think? You're a policeman! You're trained to . . .

GROBBELAAR: To kill girls? Is that what you're saying?

ROSA: Please go, Grobbelaar, we can sort it all out tomorrow.

GROBBELAAR: Haven't you noticed I don't carry a gun, Miss Rosa? I've never carried a gun on the island. I only once shot a gun, when I was at the charge office in Somerset West. There was a robber on Mrs Nellen's farm. I shot in the air. I don't know how to kill, Miss Rosa. I pray to God that I never have to do it, but if I have to do it in the line of duty, I will do it, Miss Rosa. Just like you teach lies because it's your duty.

ROSA: I do not teach lies! I have given my life to the education of our children, and what I teach them is the truth! How dare you accuse me of lies!

GROBBELAAR: You lie about your boyfriend.

(*Pause.*)

ROSA: What the hell do you know about my boyfriend? What did she tell you?

GROBBELAAR: Oh, Miss Karin never tells me anything. Miss Karin is scared of you, Miss Rosa. I think she's scared you might hurt her.

ROSA: Don't tar me with your brush, cop!

GROBBELAAR: I know you punish Miss Karin when she doesn't let you have your way. You keep her here away from the city, because you tell her how sick she will be on the boat.

ROSA: She gets seasick ...

GROBBELAAR: Only because you tell her to. There's nothing wrong with her.

ROSA: I don't really feel like this talk, Grobbelaar. It's been a hard day.

GROBBELAAR: The boyfriend from Johannesburg? I know you had one, long ago, Miss Rosa, before you came here to be a teacher; you had a boyfriend who was going out with another girl who was your best friend. And all the time you never knew they were in love till they were in that car smash. Shame. Nice friends you had.

ROSA: He still writes to me. I have letters!

GROBBELAAR: Which you write yourself and post them to yourself in Cape Town and get the post yourself so that Miss

Karin can't see the postmark is Cape Town and not Jo'burg ...

ROSA: Stop ... stop ... STOP!

GROBBELAAR: It's OK. Miss Karin's asleep. She can't hear. You gave her one of your special pills.

ROSA: You listen in?

GROBBELAAR: When I fixed your house, I added a few wires. Don't worry, Miss Rosa, you're not a threat to national security, just something that makes us laugh at the office.

ROSA: You laugh at me?

GROBBELAAR: You tell some good jokes. And those sex stories you tell Miss Karin? Good. Not accurate, but funny.

ROSA: You bastard!

GROBBELAAR: Don't start on names again, Miss Rosa. Murderer and raper is enough for one day. But it's OK, Miss Rosa, as you said, it's been a hard day. Where's the Kaffir girl?

ROSA: Sleeping in Karin's bed.

GROBBELAAR: Jisis, you'll do anything to get what you want. What's it this time? New coat of paint for the house? You put a Kaffir in her bed for what *you* want, and you know how she feels about the Kaffir girl's father and how frightened she is of anything to do with them.

ROSA: I was just doing what your office told me to do ...

(*She looks beaten, tired. The audience is aware that* KARIN *is listening, while* ROSA *and* GROBBELAAR *are unaware of it.*)

GROBBELAAR: *Ja*. Well, I just wanted to check that everything is OK here. It's not part of my duties, it's just that I feel you two might feel safer knowing someone cares.

ROSA: I'm sorry about what I said to you ...

GROBBELAAR: *Ja*, OK. (*He turns at the door.*) Oh, *ja*, by the way, Miss Rosa? Did Miss Karin give you my message?

ROSA: Message?

GROBBELAAR: About the function. I came round and she gave me a peanut-butter sandwich and I told her I wanted to take you the function.

ROSA: Me? Go with you? To your function?

GROBBELAAR: You'll enjoy it, Miss Rosa. And who knows, maybe

the day after the function Miss Karin might even hear that she got that job she wants so much. Who knows, hey, Miss Rosa?
(*Pause.*)

ROSA: How much do you know?

GROBBELAAR: No, I'm just a policeman, Miss Rosa, I don't know nothing.
(*Pause.*)

ROSA: Is it formal?

GROBBELAAR: Hey?

ROSA: Your function? A long dress?

GROBBELAAR: Jisis, you've got a long dress? Hell, that's nice, Miss Rosa. *Ja*, wear a long dress. It's formal, *ja*.
(*He is now very familiar with her. Goes close. She recoils but controls her feelings.*)

GROBBELAAR: You'll like it. We can dance. Walk on the beach in the searchlights.

ROSA: The wind will blow.

GROBBELAAR: We'll make a plan. Cheer up, the Kaffir girl will be out of here tomorrow and then things will go back to like always.

ROSA: Like always?

GROBBELAAR: Let me cheer you up with a joke I heard today. You can tell it to Miss Karin, say you made it up yourself. I won't split on you. OK? There's this husband and wife living on a farm there past nowhere and nothing. Alone. The two. Together. No TV. So she gets pregnant. Her husband must go to the town there far away to get a ... what is it? Babycatcher...

ROSA: Midwife.

GROBBELAAR: *Ja*, midwife. So he gets on his bicycle and rides for hours and miles to the *dorp* and tells the midwife she must come! So she gets into her little car and goes. And he must get back on the bike and *sukkels* his way back to the farm. But when he gets there –

ROSA: She's dead.

GROBBELAAR: No, Miss Rosa, she's not dead. Have you heard this joke before in a different way?

ROSA: No.

GROBBELAAR: Oh. Anyway, the midwife says, 'No. Hurry back to town and get the doctor, because there's a problem.' You know, with her woman's parts. Anyway, so the poor Boer goes all the way back to the dorp on the bicycle and gets the doctor and says, 'Hurry, Doctor.' So the doctor gets into his Mercedes and drives to the farm. And the poor husband has to struggle all the way back again on the bicycle. Hell, I can just see it on the dust-roads and up and down *koppies*. Anyway, he gets home, and what does the doctor say? 'The water's broken.' And the poor husband cries, 'Hell no, I'm not going back for the plumber!'

(*He laughs.* ROSA *has no reaction.*)

GROBBELAAR: The water, Miss Rosa? You know, with the baby coming and all ... did you understand it? (*He goes closer to her. Touches her.*) It's OK, I'll explain it to you at the function. Good-night, Rosa.

(*He kisses her. She breaks away from him as* SIBI *walks in holding a blanket round her.* KARIN *still pretends to sleep.*)

SIBI: Jisis, Boer, can't you keep your voice down, there are Kaffirs trying to sleep in here!

ROSA: He was just leaving ...

SIBI: I heard. You OK, Rosa?

ROSA: Shhhh, Karin's sleeping ...

GROBBELAAR: They'll come and fetch you early, 'Miss Makhale'. As a special favour we'll let you see your father and then you go by helicopter straight across to the airport and then on a plane back to where you came from.

SIBI: Where I come from I can really identify with the farmer on his bicycle. Thank you, '*Meneer* Grobbelaar' – see you on the battlefield.

GROBBELAAR: I'll be looking out for you.

SIBI: And I'll have a nice new tyre ready just for you.

(GROBBELAAR *smiles at* ROSA, *who looks away. He peers down at* KARIN *and nods. Puts his finger to his lips.*)

GROBBELAAR: Shhhh.

(*He exits.*)

SIBI: You don't have to go to that function.
ROSA: I know.
SIBI: Will you?
ROSA: I don't want to die a virgin . . . I don't know . . . Maybe if I go with him, Karin will get . . .
SIBI: Shhhh.
(*She indicates that they may be bugged.*)
ROSA: Oh . . . I . . . er . . . want to go to sleep now . . .
SIBI: I'll leave very early. I'll also have to sort out my life tomorrow.
ROSA: Good luck.
SIBI: You too.
(*Pause.*)
ROSA: That white man. Did he rape you?
SIBI: No. He loved me.
(*She exits.* ROSA *tries to control tears. Turns to the window and doesn't see* KARIN *sit up and look at her.*)
ROSA: God, it's not fair . . . Is there nobody out there who will love me?
(*Pause.* ROSA *cries. The wind wails outside.* KARIN *lies down again and pretends to wake up.* ROSA *pulls herself together and blows her nose.*)
KARIN: Oh . . . oh, what's happening . . . Rosa, is that you? Gosh, I really slept like the dead!
ROSA: It's the pill . . . why are you awake? Did we wake you?
KARIN: We? Who was here?
ROSA: Nobody.
KARIN: Do you have a cold?
ROSA: Hay fever. The sand . . .
KARIN: Well, I'm going to sleep again. It's nearly tomorrow.
ROSA: Thank God.
KARIN: Rosa?
ROSA: What is it?
KARIN: You can lie down here for a bit, if you want to. The view is so beautiful.
ROSA: It's pitch dark.
KARIN: Just imagine.

ACT TWO

ROSA: Just for a while, OK?
KARIN: *Ja*, OK.
   (ROSA *slides on to the sofa next to* KARIN, *who arranges the duvet over them both. Pause.*)
ROSA: Mind your head.
KARIN: Why?
ROSA: It's in the way of the lighthouse. That's better.
KARIN: Sorry, hey. (*Pause.*) Rosa?
ROSA: What is it?
KARIN: Do you think it will all be OK tomorrow?
ROSA: *Ja*.
KARIN: Promise?
ROSA: *Ja*, unless the wind blows again.
KARIN: Oh God, I hope not.
ROSA: Let's see what happens, OK?
KARIN: OK.
   (*Pause.*)
ROSA: Night, Karin.
KARIN: Good-night, Rosa.
   (*Silence in the house. The wind wails around it.* KARIN *and* ROSA *stare out into the darkness.*)

THE END

Glossary

amandla:	power; black nationalist call of freedom
assegai:	slender tribal spear
Boer:	Dutch or Dutch-descended South African; also slang for Afrikaner
boerewors:	local spicy sausage
braaivleis:	to fry meat, barbecue
dorp:	small town or village
drek/drekkie:	rubbish/rubbishy
Kaffir:	abusive term for black person
Karoo:	vast area of barren semi-desert between Cape Town and Johannesburg, sparsely populated
koppies:	small hills
kraal:	enclosed cluster of huts
laager:	encampment; enclosed protective place
Meneer:	Mister
né:	isn't that so?
panga:	large broad-bladed knife, like a machete
poep:	fart
se gat:	his arse (pronounced with a guttural 'g' at the back of the throat)
shame:	expression of either pity or affection
sis:	word of disapproval
sukkels:	struggles
veld:	open country
Vrystaat:	the province of the Orange Free State; also an Afrikaans cry of freedom
Xhosa	one of the indigenous black tribes of the Cape Province and their language

FOR THE BEST IN PAPERBACKS, LOOK FOR THE 🐧

In every corner of the world, on every subject under the sun, Penguin represents quality and variety – the very best in publishing today.

For complete information about books available from Penguin – including Pelicans, Puffins, Peregrines and Penguin Classics – and how to order them, write to us at the appropriate address below. Please note that for copyright reasons the selection of books varies from country to country.

In the United Kingdom: Please write to *Dept E.P., Penguin Books Ltd, Harmondsworth, Middlesex, UB7 0DA*

If you have any difficulty in obtaining a title, please send your order with the correct money, plus ten per cent for postage and packaging, to *PO Box No 11, West Drayton, Middlesex*

In the United States: Please write to *Dept BA, Penguin, 299 Murray Hill Parkway, East Rutherford, New Jersey 07073*

In Canada: Please write to *Penguin Books Canada Ltd, 2801 John Street, Markham, Ontario L3R 1B4*

In Australia: Please write to the *Marketing Department, Penguin Books Australia Ltd, P.O. Box 257, Ringwood, Victoria 3134*

In New Zealand: Please write to the *Marketing Department, Penguin Books (NZ) Ltd, Private Bag, Takapuna, Auckland 9*

In India: Please write to *Penguin Overseas Ltd, 706 Eros Apartments, 56 Nehru Place, New Delhi, 110019*

In Holland: Please write to *Penguin Books Nederland B.V., Postbus 195, NL–1380AD Weesp, Netherlands*

In Germany: Please write to *Penguin Books Ltd, Friedrichstrasse 10–12, D–6000 Frankfurt Main 1, Federal Republic of Germany*

In Spain: Please write to *Longman Penguin España, Calle San Nicolas 15, E–28013 Madrid, Spain*

In France: Please write to *Penguin Books Ltd, 39 Rue de Montmorency, F-75003, Paris, France*

In Japan: Please write to *Longman Penguin Japan Co Ltd, Yamaguchi Building, 2-12-9 Kanda Jimbocho, Chiyoda-Ku, Tokyo 101, Japan*

FOR THE BEST IN PAPERBACKS, LOOK FOR THE

A SELECTION OF FICTION AND NON-FICTION

The Rebel Angels   Robertson Davies

A glittering extravaganza of wit, scatology, saturnalia, mysticism and erudite vaudeville. 'He's the kind of writer who makes you want to nag your friends until they read him so that they can share the pleasure' – *Observer*. 'His novels will be recognized with the very best works of this century' – J. K. Galbraith in *The New York Times Book Review*

Still Life   A. S. Byatt

In this sequel to her much praised *The Virgin in the Garden*, A. S. Byatt illuminates the inevitable conflicts between ambition and domesticity, confinement and self-fulfilment while providing an incisive observation of cultural life in England during the 1950s. 'Affords enormous and continuous pleasure' – Anita Brookner in the *Standard*

Heartbreak Hotel   Gabrielle Burton

'If *Heartbreak Hotel* doesn't make you laugh, perhaps you are no longer breathing. Check all vital signs of life, and read this book!' – Rita Mae Brown. 'A novel to take us into the next century, heads high and flags flying' – Fay Weldon

August in July   Carlo Gébler

On the eve of the Royal Wedding, as the nation prepares for celebration, August Slemic's world prepares to fall apart. 'There is no question but that he must now be considered a novelist of major importance' – *Daily Telegraph*. 'A meticulous study, done with great sympathy . . . a thoroughly honest and loving book' – *Financial Times*

The News from Ireland   William Trevor

'An ability to enchant as much as chill has made Trevor unquestionably one of our greatest short-story writers' – *The Times*. 'A masterly collection' – *Daily Telegraph*. 'Extremely impressive . . . of his stature as a writer there can be no question' – *New Statesman*

FOR THE BEST IN PAPERBACKS, LOOK FOR THE 🐧

A SELECTION OF FICTION AND NON-FICTION

A Confederacy of Dunces John Kennedy Toole

In this Pulitzer-Prize-winning novel, in the bulky figure of Ignatius J. Reilly, an immortal comic character is born. 'I succumbed, stunned and seduced . . . it is a masterwork of comedy' – *The New York Times*

The Labyrinth of Solitude Octavio Paz

Nine remarkable essays by Mexico's finest living poet: 'A profound and original book . . . with Lowry's *Under the Volcano* and Eisenstein's *Que Viva Mexico!*, *The Labyrinth of Solitude* completes the trinity of masterworks about the spirit of modern Mexico' – *Sunday Times*

Falconer John Cheever

Ezekiel Farragut, fratricide with a heroin habit, comes to Falconer Correctional Facility. His freedom is enclosed, his view curtailed by iron bars. But he is a man, none the less, and the vice, misery and degradation of prison change a man . . .

The Memory of War and Children in Exile: (Poems 1968–83) James Fenton

'James Fenton is a poet I find myself again and again wanting to praise' – *Listener*. 'His assemblages bring with them tragedy, comedy, love of the world's variety, and the sadness of its moral blight' – *Observer*

The Bloody Chamber Angela Carter

In tales that glitter and haunt – strange nuggets from a writer whose wayward pen spills forth stylish, erotic, nightmarish jewels of prose – the old fairy stories live and breathe again, subtly altered, subtly changed.

Cannibalism and the Common Law A. W. Brian Simpson

In 1884 Tod Dudley and Edwin Stephens were sentenced to death for killing their shipmate in order to eat him. A. W. Brian Simpson unfolds the story of this macabre case in 'a marvellous rangy, atmospheric, complicated book . . . an irresistible blend of sensation and scholarship' – Jonathan Raban in the *Sunday Times*

FOR THE BEST IN PAPERBACKS, LOOK FOR THE 🐧

A SELECTION OF FICTION AND NON-FICTION

Cat's Grin François Maspero

'Reflects in some measure the experience of every French person . . . evacuees, peasants, Resistance fighters, *collabos* . . . Maspero's painfully truthful book helps to ensure that it never seems commonplace' – *Literary Review*

The Moronic Inferno Martin Amis

'This is really good reading and sharp, crackling writing. Amis has a beguiling mixture of confidence and courtesy, and most of his literary judgements – often twinned with interviews – seem sturdy, even when caustic, without being bitchy for the hell of it' – *Guardian*

In Custody Anita Desai

Deven, a lecturer in a small town in Northern India, is resigned to a life of mediocrity and empty dreams. When asked to interview the greatest poet of Delhi, Deven discovers a new kind of dignity, both for himself and his dreams.

Parallel Lives Phyllis Rose

In this study of five famous Victorian marriages, including that of John Ruskin and Effie Gray, Phyllis Rose probes our inherited myths and assumptions to make us look again at what we expect from our marriages.

Lamb Bernard MacLaverty

In the Borstal run by Brother Benedict, boys are taught a little of God and a lot of fear. Michael Lamb, one of the brothers, runs away and takes a small boy with him. As the outside world closes in around them, Michael is forced to an uncompromising solution.

FOR THE BEST IN PAPERBACKS, LOOK FOR THE

A CHOICE OF PENGUINS

Adieux   Simone de Beauvoir

This 'farewell to Sartre' by his life-long companion is a 'true labour of love' (the *Listener*) and 'an extraordinary achievement' (*New Statesman*).

British Society 1914–45   John Stevenson

A major contribution to the Pelican Social History of Britain, which 'will undoubtedly be the standard work for students of modern Britain for many years to come' – *The Times Educational Supplement*

The Pelican History of Greek Literature   Peter Levi

A remarkable survey covering all the major writers from Homer to Plutarch, with brilliant translations by the author, one of the leading poets of today.

Art and Literature   Sigmund Freud

Volume 14 of the Pelican Freud Library contains Freud's major essays on Leonardo, Michelangelo and Dostoyevsky, plus shorter pieces on Shakespeare, the nature of creativity and much more.

A History of the Crusades   Sir Steven Runciman

This three-volume history of the events which transferred world power to Western Europe – and founded Modern History – has been universally acclaimed as a masterpiece.

A Night to Remember   Walter Lord

The classic account of the sinking of the *Titanic*. 'A stunning book, incomparably the best on its subject and one of the most exciting books of this or any year' – *The New York Times*

FOR THE BEST IN PAPERBACKS, LOOK FOR THE 🐧

A CHOICE OF PENGUINS

The Informed Heart   Bruno Bettelheim

Bettelheim draws on his experience in concentration camps to illuminate the dangers inherent in all mass societies in this profound and moving masterpiece.

God and the New Physics   Paul Davies

Can science, now come of age, offer a surer path to God than religion? This 'very interesting' (*New Scientist*) book suggests it can.

Modernism   Malcolm Bradbury and James McFarlane (eds.)

A brilliant collection of essays dealing with all aspects of literature and culture for the period 1890–1930 – from Apollinaire and Brecht to Yeats and Zola.

Rise to Globalism   Stephen E. Ambrose

A clear, up-to-date and well-researched history of American foreign policy since 1938, Volume 8 of the Pelican History of the United States.

The Waning of the Middle Ages   Johan Huizinga

A magnificent study of life, thought and art in 14th and 15th century France and the Netherlands, long established as a classic.

The Penguin Dictionary of Psychology   Arthur S. Reber

Over 17,000 terms from psychology, psychiatry and related fields are given clear, concise and modern definitions.

FOR THE BEST IN PAPERBACKS, LOOK FOR THE 🐧

PENGUIN INTERNATIONAL POETS

Anna Akhmatova Translated by D. M. Thomas

Anna Akhmatova is not only Russia's finest woman poet but perhaps the finest in the history of Western Culture.

Fernando Pessoa

'I have sought for his shade in those Edwardian cafés in Lisbon which he haunted, for he was Lisbon's Cavafy or Verlaine' – Cyril Connolly in the *Sunday Times*

Yehuda Amichai Translated by Chana Bloch and Stephen Mitchell

'A truly major poet . . . there's a depth, breadth and weighty momentum in these subtle and delicate poems of his' – Ted Hughes

Czeslaw Milosz

Czeslaw Milosz received the Nobel Prize for Literature in 1980. 'One of the greatest poets of our time, perhaps the greatest' – Joseph Brodsky

To Urania Joseph Brodsky
Winner of the 1987 Nobel Prize for Literature

Exiled from the Soviet Union in 1972, Joseph Brodsky has been universally acclaimed as the most talented Russian poet of his generation.

Philippe Jaccottet

This volume, contains the first translations into English of the poetry of Philippe Jaccottet, 'one of the finest European poets of the century'.

Osip Mandelstam Translated by Clarence Brown and W. S. Merwin

Like his friends Pasternak and Akhmatova, Mandelstam, through his work, bore witness to the plight of Russia under Stalin – for which he paid with his life.

Pablo Neruda

From the poet-explorer of his early years to the poet-historian of 'my thin country', Neruda's personal turning point came when he was posted to Barcelona as Chilean consul just before the Spanish Civil War.

FOR THE BEST IN PAPERBACKS, LOOK FOR THE

PENGUIN INTERNATIONAL WRITERS

Titles already published or in preparation

Gamal Al-Ghitany	**Zayni Barakat**
Isabel Allende	**Eva Luna**
Wang Anyi	**Baotown**
Joseph Brodsky	**Marbles: A Play in Three Acts**
Doris Dorrie	**Love, Pain and the Whole Damn Thing**
Shusaku Endo	**Scandal**
	Wonderful Fool
Ida Fink	**A Scrap of Time**
Daniele Del Giudice	**Lines of Light**
Miklos Haraszti	**The Velvet Prison**
Ivan Klima	**My First Loves**
	A Summer Affair
Jean Levi	**The Chinese Emperor**
Harry Mulisch	**Last Call**
Cees Nooteboom	**The Dutch Mountains**
	A Song of Truth and Semblance
Milorad Pavic	**Dictionary of the Khazars (Male)**
	Dictionary of the Khazars (Female)
Luise Rinser	**Prison Journal**
A. Solzhenitsyn	**Matryona's House and Other Stories**
	One Day in the Life of Ivan Denisovich
Tatyana Tolstoya	**On the Golden Porch and Other Stories**
Elie Wiesel	**Twilight**
Zhang Xianliang	**Half of Man is Woman**

FOR THE BEST IN PAPERBACKS, LOOK FOR THE 🐧

PLAYS IN PENGUIN

Edward Albee **Who's Afraid of Virginia Woolf?**
Alan Ayckbourn **The Norman Conquests**
Bertolt Brecht **Parables for the Theatre (The Good Woman of Setzuan/The Caucasian Chalk Circle)**
Anton Checkhov **Plays (The Cherry Orchard/The Three Sisters/Ivanov/The Seagull/Uncle Vanya)**
Vladimir Gubaryev **Sarcophagus**
Henrik Ibsen **Hedda Gabler/Pillar of Society/The Wild Duck**
Eugène Ionesco **Absurd Drama (Rhinoceros/The Chair/The Lesson)**
Ben Jonson **Three Comedies (Volpone/The Alchemist/Bartholomew Fair)**
D. H. Lawrence **Three Plays (The Collier's Friday Night/The Daughter-in-Law/The Widowing of Mrs Holroyd)**
Federico García Lorca **Three Tragedies**
Arthur Miller **Death of a Salesman**
John Mortimer **A Voyage Round My Father/What Shall We Tell Caroline?/The Dock Brief**
J. B. Priestly **Time and the Conways/I Have Been Here Before/An Inspector Calls/The Linden Tree**
Peter Shaffer **Amadeus/Equus**
Bernard Shaw **Plays Pleasant (Arms and the Man/Candida/The Man of Destiny/You Never Can Tell)**
Sophocles **Three Theban Plays (Oedipus the King/Antigone/Oedipus at Colonus)**
Arnold Wesker **The Wesker Trilogy (Chicken Soup with Barley/Roots/I'm Talking about Jerusalem)**
Oscar Wilde **Plays (Lady Windermere's Fan/A Woman of No Importance/An Ideal Husband/The Importance of Being Earnest/Salome)**
Thornton Wilder **Our Town/The Skin of Our Teeth/The Matchmaker**
Tennessee Williams **Sweet Bird of Youth/A Streetcar Named Desire/The Glass Menagerie**